Casa Hogar Los Angelitos was founded by a magnetic, sincere, and charismatic person—Nancy Nystrom.

Her purpose as an altruist has been to reach out to help these less fortunate children [who are] orphaned and from dysfunctional families. *Voilá!* Nancy is a skilled, successful, and gracious lady who pursues this task. I have been by her side through good times and bad. She has never lost her drive or her faith.

God bless you, Nancy!

Eileen Deena "Bonnie" Sumlin
LICDA — Masters in Special Education and Languages
Director of HELP!
Auxiliary U.S. Consul, Guadalajara, Jalisco
Past President, Mexican Red Cross, Manzanillo, Colima

EACH DAY
A PORTION

Each day is a portion of my life...

some seem waste, some gain...

but each a portion that cannot be replaced.

Each Day a Portion

ISBN 978-0-615-54299-7

Published by
The Children's Foundation

THE CHILDREN'S FOUNDATION
P.O. Box 1443
Loveland, Colorado USA 80539
www.TCFcares.org

Printed in the United States of America

Book and cover design, editing, and layout by
Martha W. Nichols/aMuse Productions®

EACH DAY
A PORTION

NANCY NYSTROM

THE CHILDREN'S FOUNDATION

FOR THE CHILDREN...

...who endure abuse or abandonment by their families and society. For those who suffer the absence of support to meet their basic needs, predisposing them to lives of poverty, exploitation, crime, drugs, and prostitution.

Without the social structure for emotional nurturing or the encouragement and tools to succeed in school, these children face lives of desperation without hope, a future of closed doors.

Casa Hogar Los Angelitos—an orphanage and children's home located in Manzanillo, Mexico, founded in 1995—officially opened its doors to orphaned, abandoned, desperately poor, and abused children in June 1996.

These children come with nothing; in their world they are nothing; they have nowhere to turn for their basic needs, but at this oasis of refuge, Casa Hogar Los Angelitos, they receive comprehensive care. They are loved, respected, and nurtured, and they learn that they are very special.

This story is not only my story—it is bits and pieces of many stories. They're stories about that work, those children, and the people who have put into action their compassion and conviction to help the children. This is everyone's story.

Nancy Nystrom
2012

It is not ourselves, but our responsibilities that we should take seriously.

Author unknown

ACKNOWLEDGMENTS

Thank you to all those who have gone before me, faced the trials and struggles of life, and stood firm with conviction and determination.

To my five beautiful children—Eric, Fred, Dyanne, Christie, and Rob—who gave me the joy of childhood and life, even in my darkest moments. You were the reason I kept going even when I didn't know how I could. Through your magical personalities, each different, you gave me life and made me love all children.

To Naomi Cotton, who is now in her nineties, Farrell Brock, who has passed away, and all the other wonderful ladies at West 14th Avenue Baptist Church who showed me how to behave like a lady and who made me feel special and loved. I can never be as gracious and lovely as they were, but they provided an example that I have kept in my heart even to this day.

To Brother and Mrs. Hollems, pastors during my young life, who spent countless hours at my mother and grandmother's house always talking, teaching, and quietly living the Word of God. They gave me a love for the scriptures and a true and humble example of what it meant to be a follower of Christ.

To my two teachers, Margaret Mallot and Jewel Gibson, who believed in me and my potential. They pushed me into confidence and determination to believe that I could do anything I set my heart to do. They were some of the first women liberators who gave us the courage to believe, as the words in the Helen Reddy song: "I am strong; I am invincible; I am woman."

To my patient and loyal friends who waded through the beginnings of this little book and encouraged me to continue even when I doubted the value or benefit of continuing: LeaAnna, Jan, Marilyn, Janice, and Melanie—thank you.

To my mother, who suffered unbelievable tragedies and disappoint-ments in her life, yet she maintained and even grew in her faith, becoming one of the most knowledgeable Bible teachers I have known. Mother, you were my hero.

To my friends: to Monica Welter de O'Farrill, who gave her name and support so that we could complete the legal paperwork we needed in Mexico; to Lic. Rafael de la Colina Rosecrans, our attorney, now deceased, who gave eight years of legal counsel; to Lidia Rodriguez Montes de Oca, who was the first person to join our board—at the very beginning. Lidia carries the weight of being our legal representative and has worked con-tinually and diligently from the beginning to make this vision a reality, to help keep me out of trouble, and so much more. It would have been impossible to wade through all the storms and tribulations without Lidia; and to all those who contributed and shared in this vision and dream to help the children of Mexico.

And finally, to my husband Dave, always the protector and the provider, who didn't want me to expose myself to the world through this book. He has kept me safe and secure throughout these last thirty years. He has loved me even when I wasn't lovable; he has stood by me, even when I couldn't stand; he has been patient, even when he didn't understand what was going on; and because of his strength, support, and determination, this work has been made possible. Thank you, sweetheart.

PREFACE

My goal in writing this little book is to help people become aware of the plight of children, the problems in Mexico that we ignore, and the tremendous need for help through operations and projects such as Casa Hogar Los Angelitos.

This book is about how all of our past, as well as the people of the past, the good and the bad, can give us strength, experience, courage, and determination to overcome adversity and accomplish tasks that would otherwise seem impossible. It is about the history of me and the history of Casa Hogar Los Angelitos—the challenges, the heartbreak, the successes, and just a few of the many stories.

It touches on the positive and negative effects of changes and experiences in our lives, and the spiritual journey that can lead to a sense of purpose that connects us to a realization that we are all on this earth for a purpose.

I hope that I have presented this correctly, so that this story might inspire some, interest others, and encourage understanding as well as help from more people.

NOTE: As in many nonfiction books, some names have been changed for understandable reasons.

FOREWORD I

Within the first hour of my arrival at Casa Hogar Los Angelitos (CHLA), I was in a van with Nancy, a handful of teens from the orphanage, and a driver who was taking us to a remote migrant worker camp. After a long drive down a dusty dirt road, we arrived at a camp of about forty people, including women and children, sharing tents made of sticks and garbage bags. There was no running water, no toilets, and a level of extreme poverty that I had seen before only in Africa. These families had come from the south to work the fields outside of Manzanillo, Mexico, planting and picking vegetables. Families, including children, would work in the heat of the fields all week, sometimes 12 hours a day, to make the weekly equivalent of thirty dollars (U.S.).

Nancy had heard about the plight of these children several years previous and was making her regular delivery of food and supplies and an offer to educate the kids. I watched as she greeted each of the children, many covered in dirt, with hugs and spoke to them in fluent Spanish. As our driver worked to repair the electric generator that Nancy had brought the previous week, I observed how she built relationships with the children's mothers, assessing their needs and offering help. What I remember the most from that first day was her smile and laugh. There are some things that transcend race, class, and nationality.

I walked into CHLA for the first time in early February 2011. I was immediately impressed by the beauty of the physical space. The orphanage is set on a quiet piece of property in the small town of Salagua just north of Manzanillo. The well-maintained buildings are positioned around a large Spanish-inspired courtyard full of flowers and mango trees. I checked in at the office using my best college Spanish, and a young man pointed me toward Nancy. As I walked into the courtyard I couldn't miss her. The tall, fair-skinned, red-headed woman from Colorado stood out in the group of brown-skinned children she was embracing and talking to. She greeted me with a big smile and told me that she was glad I was there. Behind the smile, I noticed a look of caution in her eyes. It is the look that mothers have when protecting their children. Even though I have credentials, a professional history of working with kids, and had completed the extensive background check, I knew that I would have to earn her trust. A few weeks later I learned that Mexico is a prime destination for sexual tourism, a horrific practice where [mostly] men from the U.S. and Canada come to Mexico to sexually exploit underage children. Since many of the children at CHLA have histories of sexual abuse, sexual assault, and prostitution, Nancy has every reason to be cautious.

I was granted a university sabbatical during spring semester 2011. Having worked as a social worker for 20 years, I searched for an organization where I could volunteer my clinical skills and learn more about child trauma. Casa Hogar Los Angelitos came highly recommended as a program that was successful at serving "difficult-to-place" children in Mexico. I was privileged to spend my sabbatical observing and learning from Nancy, building relationships with the kids and working with the staff at the orphanage. Nancy and her team at CHLA were generous with their time and knowledge. I tried to quickly absorb their wisdom.

I discovered many reasons for the success of CHLA while I was there. They have dedicated staff, passionate volunteers, and a holistic approach to child development. A surprising finding, and maybe the strongest reason for their success, was the extensive use of expressive arts in the daily lives of the children there. Nancy instinctively began using expressive arts at the orphanage when she started it more than 15 years ago. Children receive instruction in music and have regular access to instruments. They train and participate in a highly skilled and prestigious local troupe of dancers that performs traditional Mexican dances in local, national, and international venues. The kids have access to donated art supplies and regularly draw and paint. Many of the children participate in creative writing, journaling, and poetry. Expressive arts are integrated into each stage of the child's development. When I told her there was a growing body of research showing the healing power of art, she smiled, as if to say "I knew that." For her, it was a natural way to engage children and help them recover.

During my first week at CHLA, Nancy invited me to coffee with four teenage boys from the orphanage. The high-school-aged boys dazzled me with their intelligence and charm. They are beating the odds and succeeding despite the many adversities that had been placed before them. The boys have dreams of being doctors, lawyers, and firemen. Each is doing well at school and has begun to consider college. In her research, Linda

Sanford found that victims of childhood trauma eventually come to the proverbial fork in the road. Some go on to be survivors while others go down a different path—of violence and self-destruction. The survivors seemed to have found a way to move toward healing by finding a loving relationship that provides consistency, patience, kindness, and hope. Watching Nancy's steadfast love for these boys, I saw how they had transformed and become strong in the broken places. When they entered CHLA years ago, they were diamonds in the rough. That night I saw them sparkle.

I was honored when [Nancy] asked me to read her life story. I now have a better idea of why she strives tirelessly to better the lives of abused and neglected children. Her personal journey is a roller coaster ride of heartbreak and joy, success and setback, love and loss, and a heroic journey through the dark night of the soul. As you read stories of her work at CHLA, you will quickly feel her love and devotion to the hundreds of children who think of her as their mother. Given the obstacles she continually has to overcome to serve these children in Mexico, I couldn't help but ask her why she still does it. Her answer was clear and direct. "It is the place where God wants me to be." Martin Luther King, Jr., wrote that "Faith is taking the first step even when you don't see the whole staircase." Nancy continues to climb when others would have given up or retreated.

In his book, *Tattoos on the Heart: The Power of Boundless Compassion*, Father Gregory Boyle said, "Compassion is not a relationship between the healer and the wounded. It's a covenant between equals. Compassion is always, at its most authentic, about a shift from the cramped world of self-preoccupation into a more expansive place of fellowship, of true kinship.... Compassion isn't just about feeling the pain of others; it's about bringing them in toward yourself. If we love what God loves, then, in compassion, margins get erased." Through her daily actions, Nancy models compassion. She has gone far beyond funding and administering a program for needy children. She has true kinship with the children at CHLA. Because of her unwavering belief in every child there, the children slowly begin to believe in themselves. She attends school graduations and dance performances like a proud parent, showering each child with praise and affection. She holds their hands when they are sick and cries with them when they are pain. Her love is tactile. Children at CHLA crave the attention and affection that she provides abundantly. For many, it's the first secure attachment in their life.

Day after day, Nancy rolls up her sleeves and enters into the lives of the abandoned and maltreated. She creates a safe and nurturing environment that provides physical safety, emotional security, predictability, consistency, and unconditional love. Philip Zimbardo wrote, "Heroes circulate the life force of goodness in our veins."

Nancy's story is a reminder that we all have the obligation and responsibility to care for and serve one another. I am grateful for all that she continues to teach me. Real heroes still exist. As the light grows within each of us, the dark places become smaller. Nancy continues to radiate warmth and brightness in all of her relationships. She offers hope to the hopeless and direction to the lost. As we each navigate our lives and search for meaning, Nancy is a shining star guiding us toward true north.

Don Phelps, Ph.D., LCSW
August 2011
Chicago, Illinois

FOREWORD II

When a child is brought to Casa Hogar Los Angelitos as a result of the inability of the parents to safely care for their child due to abuse, neglect, poverty, absence, dangerous lifestyle, and other tragic reasons, this child will be given an opportunity very unique to casa hogars worldwide. This child will not only be given a safe home, food, clothing, and basic essentials, he/she will be given the opportunity to grow in an environment where his/her physical, social, psychological, educational, and spiritual needs are recognized and met.

Children can enter CHLA as young as infants and will be a part of the CHLA family until they are adults functioning successfully in the world. In addition to focus on education there is a strong focus on activities and opportunities that enhance individual self-esteem, teach discipline, encourage social interaction, and build pride of self and of their culture. Many of the children are very gifted and talented and do well in school. If a child has special needs, these are recognized and addressed. The staff is professional and well-trained in their fields...as a caretaker (housemother), social worker, psychologist, educational tutor, etc.

The cost of running an organization such as Casa Hogar Los Angelitos must be covered by donations and the generosity of those who care about the children.

Dance, music, art, computer, and English-language lessons are an integral part of the daily life at CHLA. The Ballet Folklorico Casa Hogar Los Angelitos has become well-recognized here in Manzanillo and also in parts of Colorado. The children participating in this program must maintain a high academic average and participate in a demanding training schedule. Any child who wishes may join the dance and other programs. As the years go by, the little ones begin to advance in their skills to the point where they perform in front of hundreds of people. The older children coach the younger ones and encourage them. Professionals are hired to teach dance, music, art, etc. These teachers enrich the child's life and provide help for the child to feel proud of him/herself. This a huge building block for a successful future. The goal is that each child is given the opportunity to break the cycle from which he/she came. No child is "abandoned" once they reach a certain age or considered hopeless so long as they are part of the CHLA family.

Janice Morgan Babcock

Bachelor of Arts in Social Welfare, University of California, Berkeley
Masters of Arts in Psychology; Licensed Marriage and Family Therapist, California
Teaching Credentials in Elementary Education and Special Education, California

FOREWORD III

Have you ever walked inside a building and *known* something special was happening? That was the feeling I had in June 2005 as I walked through the doors of Casa Hogar Los Angelitos.

I had heard good things about the orphanage, and going to do ministry there came at the recommendation of a friend I trust. There are many worthy projects around the world where one can make a difference, and I expected Casa Hogar to be another of those good projects. I was anticipating my students would meet God through the eyes of the orphans, to do fruitful ministry, and leave wishing there was more we could do. What I did not expect was an experience that would help transform our church! Our students came back to Colorado so energized, so compelled, and so moved that adults from the church could not dismiss their experience as youthful passion but an encounter with the living God. Since that first trip, over 115 members of our mid-sized church have done ministry on site and been swept up in a movement of God. That transformative experience in Mexico has spilled over into a passion at our church for children in pain in our own neighborhood and a renewed commitment to be a difference maker in our own context. Who would have thought that 50 orphans in Mexico could help transform a church 2,500 miles away?

Casa Hogar Los Angelitos does everything in its power to end the horrific cycle of abuse and neglect. With care and love, they address the emotional, physical, educational, psychological, and spiritual needs of children. Casa Hogar is an oasis in the middle of a society without a safety net for these types of children. I am honored to be a friend, participant, and donor to the project.

At the center of it all is my good friend, Nancy Nystrom. Her passion, commitment, and heart inspires us all to give of ourselves for the sake of these children and other children in difficult circumstances. She and her husband, Dave, have sacrificed beyond measure to follow the prompting of God. I am a better person for knowing Nancy, and I trust that as you meet her in the pages of this book, you will be blessed as well.

Rev. Jeffrey S. Berg
LifeSpring Covenant Church

AUTHOR'S INTRODUCTION

THE BATTLE RAGING FOR CHILDREN

*It was a war in the heavens...the sharp, craggy lines of lightning crack-
ing the sky, crashing overhead with claps of thunder that made me cover
my face and cringe with fear. It was as if there were a battle raging between heaven and hell...right over my head.*

*If all went well, tomorrow we would finally be able to officially open
the doors to Casa Hogar Los Angelitos.*

José was one of the children who had been "working the streets"—holding diesel fuel in his mouth then swiftly lighting it as he spewed out a
stream, curling his tongue between his teeth, looking for any pesos that
people might be willing to give him.

We saw him on the streets, a little boy about 9 years old. Felipe, my as-
sistant, and I walked over to where he was "working" to invite him to the
comedor (food kitchen) to eat. It was obvious that if he continued this activity there would be long term damage to his lungs, brain, and body. We
told him that he could eat at the dining room that we had opened, but he
had to stop the dangerous diesel "spew," he looked at us, wide-eyed, and
explained, "I have to work the street because my mother sends me out
each day to earn enough money to feed my little brother and sister."

We made a deal with him, and asked to talk to his mother. He brought her
to the *comedor* the next day. I saw that she had a beautiful face, but her
black hair was full of white nits (lice eggs). She had bright lipstick and
heavy makeup on, possibly to make herself more attractive to the cross-
country truckers and other men who might be interested in her or her
companionship.

We told her that we would feed all three of her children—every day—
if she would *not* send José out on the streets anymore. She hesitantly
agreed, and the three children began coming each day at noon. Some days
José would ask for extra food to take to his mother, and we would pack up
extras to send home with him.

One day as I was leaving the *comedor* in our van, José ran out and climbed up on the running board grinning into the window, eyes wide and bright as he held on. I will always remember his words and expression as he pleadingly said, "*Ayúdame*" (help me).

I made a promise to little José (and to myself) that day which I have been determined to fulfill... "Yes, I will help you."

In June of 1996, after months of waiting, our paperwork was finally approved, and we had official permission to open the doors of an orphanage and children's home—Casa Hogar Los Angelitos—and took in our first child—little José.

The past many years of my life have been dedicated to establishing a safe and productive environment for children and youth, fueled by a vision and a spiritual journey that has brought me to this place where I am today.

It is the chain of events, beginning in my early life, even before I was born, that has brought me on this journey, a journey of hope to rescue, care for, and positively change the lives of children.

As I think of the children that we care for at Casa Hogar Los Angelitos, and the millions of others that are still out there in their pain, chains of abuse and abandonment, my thoughts wander back to my own life. While there is no comparison when compared to the horror that these children suffer, the sense of betrayal, there are glimpses, bits and pieces of sensation and pain that makes me aware of, and sensitive to the frustration, confusion, feelings of abandonment, and desperation that they suffer every day.

My life is not so different from many others, but by retracing some of the passages of the past and my childhood, the good and the bad, perhaps I can open the door of understanding of why, today, I am willing to fight for children, why they are so important, and why I believe that their tender hearts are closest to the heart of God and the most precious and valuable asset that the world has.

It is the angels of the children who are always in God's presence.

Beware that you don't despise a single one of these little ones. For I tell you
that in heaven their angels are always in the presence of my heavenly
Father.

Matthew 18:10-11 (NLT)

As I begin to write some of the stories that have brought me to this
place in life I am reminded of the expression, "Truth is stranger than fiction." Trying to document those things I have seen, events that have happened to me or around me, I am aware that there will be those who doubt
these things and question my "balance." To those people, I can say that before September 1994, I too would have questioned the credibility and san-
ity of some of these events, because at times, even to me, they seem
stranger than fiction.

We humans don't seem to understand the spiritual world. "Things of
the spirit" are part of the unknown. We tend to be afraid of the unknown
and we shut down our senses and hearts to anything that seems "too spiritual" or "too unusual." Ignoring or suppressing, we don't talk about "it,"
other than whispers or thoughts in the night, because we know someone
will look at us sideways, roll their eyes off to the left or right, and whether
they say it out loud or not, think Hmmmm. There is a tendency to catego-
rize people and experiences into boxes such as too "Charismatic," "New
Age," "weird," and even "demonic."

Yet, I believe that if everyone allowed the hidden tenderness in their
heart to be opened, paid attention to the spiritual things around them,
and had the courage to share their experiences, we would suddenly find
hundreds of thousands of people with similar "unusual" experiences.

Regardless of how others might judge, I feel compelled to document
what I believe to be true. Experiences on a path that changed my life, turning sorrow into inspiration, depression into hope, opening my spirit and
heart, through deep pain, to a personal and intimate relationship of faith
and spirit of conviction that I never would have thought possible for me.
In this effort I will try to be accurate relating some of the stories as I experienced them.

PART ONE

How do we know of feelings?
How do we measure others,
By our own valleys?
We cannot, because each capacity is a variance...

Streams
Rivers
Oceans...
Fast
Slow
Shallow
Deeper...

People are oceans, valleys, streams
Even great mountains,
Each different.
Our lives are like the mountain,
Each rock, each blade of grass, each crevice
Represents a portion of that mountain,
Together, forming the entire mountain...Life.

Nancy

We are all travelers in what John Bunyan calls "the wilderness of this world"...all, too, travelers with a donkey.

Robert Louis Stevenson

CHAPTER I

It has been tremendously difficult to write about the personal details of my life. The bad decisions, some I am still ashamed of, the unusual, the failures...and the "donkey" traveling with me that sometimes carried me and sometimes I had to carry.

It is difficult to pick and choose which to share, not wanting to expose or embarrass others or to bore people with too many details. Some experiences and memories seem too uncomfortable to even contemplate, much less expose to the world. However, my purpose for sharing sensitive areas is with the hope to inspire others to find healing and to witness that even a chipped and cracked vessel, which I consider myself to be, can be used to make a difference in this life, can have a purpose.

> God loves me all the time...the good, the bad, the ugly, and the donkey
> inside of me.
>
> Nancy

I don't presume that anyone would find my life particularly interesting to read about. When I think about all the books I've read where the authors talked about themselves, some interestingly and some boringly, I am hesitant to even approach that subject. However, having said that, I intend to give a little background of where I came from, though it seems a long time ago. Perhaps knowing where you came from helps to know how you got where you are—and where you might be going.

The real reason for beginning now is to document people, places, and things while I still have my memory function.

My mother was very active and mentally alert up until the last months before her death. Yet, a few years before she passed away, she would be talking about a photo or an experience, and I would look at the photo or think about the experience and say, "That was me, Mother, not you."

"Are you sure?" she would ask.

We tend to get times and experiences confused as we get older, combining stories that we've heard with experiences that we've had and meshing them all together. As we reach different stages of our lives, we begin to insert ourselves into situations or see ourselves in photos that didn't involve us. I want to hurry and finish this before I fall into that memory time lapse, thinking I am my mother, or worse, my daughter.

I have also inserted a few writings accumulated over the past forty years, written at various times in my life. Some relate despair; some the love and acceptance that I kept looking for; and some happened just because I liked to write.

I believe that, in addition to our parents and genetics, it is the accumulation and combination of all of our experiences and dreams that shape our lives and color our perspective. That is why all of it—the good, the bad, the ugly, and the donkey we take along with us—formed the building blocks of our lives. The past does not control our lives, but the past is part of each of us.

It is interesting to consider how we are prepared, shaped, and inspired using all those different-colored building blocks of events and experiences, some even before we are born, for challenges, or situations that we may face in our lives.

My grandfather—"Papa," as we knew him—grew up on a pea farm, where he labored in the brutally hot, dry, and dusty fields picking cotton and black-eyed peas. Papa was part of a sharecropper's family —hardscrabble—or just plain dirt farmer. His family migrated into central Texas in clapboard wagons and on river barges down the Mississippi from Missouri, then followed the coastline and finally settled outside a slightly nothing town called Tabor.

Perhaps they named the little gathering place *Tabor* because it rhymed with *labor*, which is what everyone in that area did during those days.

> *These people in Texas were similar to the "aparcero" of Mexico...the people who spend their lives laboring in the hot fields, who work for others, who share their crops, and who provide the food for the rest of society. Migrant families travel from southern Mexico—places like Guerrero, Oaxaca, and Chiapas as well as the northern border states of Mexico—bringing their entire families from the tiniest to the biggest, all working together in the blistering sun for one small fee.*
>
> *Today, here in the U.S., there are big green, red, or blue machines that move across the fields picking cotton, taking over the backbreaking daily grind of scores of workers and families. However, in Mexico and other parts of the world, most of the truck farms of cotton, tomatoes,chilies, beans, and peas still use hand laborers, called "mano de obra."*

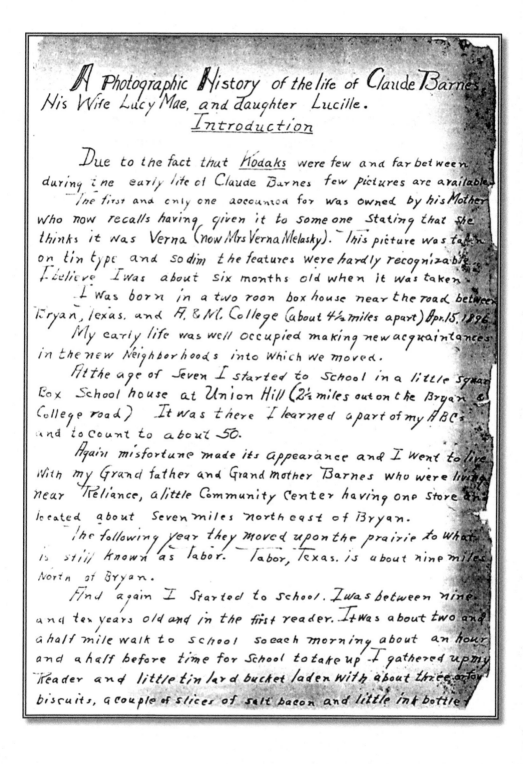

A Photographic History of the life of Claude Barnes,
His Wife Lucy Mae, and daughter Lucille.

Introduction

Due to the fact that Kodaks were few and far between
during the early life of Claude Barnes few pictures are available.
The first and only one accounted for was owned by his Mother
who now recalls having given it to some one stating that she
thinks it was Verna (now Mrs Verna Melasky). This picture was taken
on tin type and so dim the features were hardly recognizable.
I believe I was about six months old when it was taken.

I was born in a two roon box house near the road between
Bryan, Texas. and A. & M. College (about 4½ miles apart) Apr. 15, 1896.

My early life was well occupied making new acquaintances
in the new Neighborhoods into which we moved.

At the age of Seven I started to school in a little square
Box School house at Union Hill (2½ miles out on the Bryan &
College road) It was there I learned a part of my ABC's
and to count to about 50.

Again misfortune made its appearance and I went to live
with my Grand father and Grand mother Barnes who were living
near Reliance, a little Community Center having one store and
located about Seven miles north east of Bryan.

The following year they moved upon the prairie to what
is still known as Tabor. Tabor, Texas. is about nine miles
North of Bryan.

And again I started to school. I was between nine
and ten years old and in the first reader. It was about two and
a half mile walk to school so each morning about an hour
and a half before time for school to take up I gathered up my
reader and little tin lard bucket laden with about three or four
biscuits, a couple of slices of salt bacon and little ink bottle

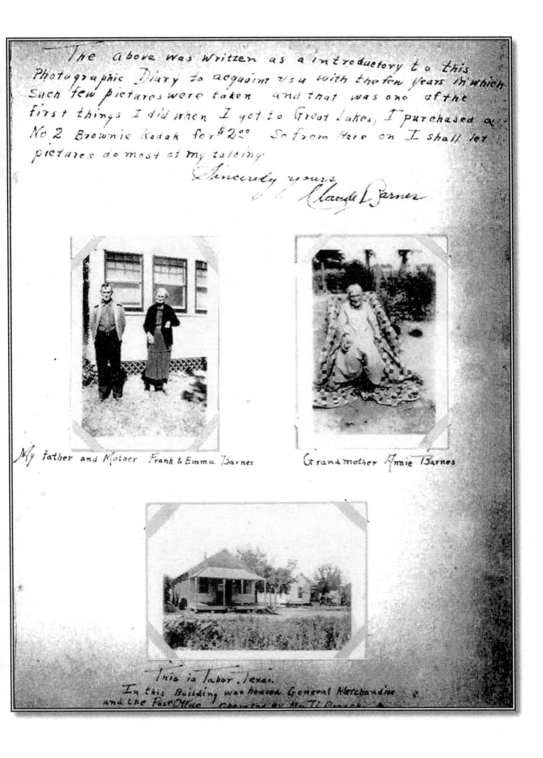

The above was written as a introductory to this Photographic Diary to acquaint you with the few years in which such few pictures were taken and that was one of the first things I did when I got to Great Lakes, I purchased a No 2 Brownie Kodak for $2.°° So from here on I shall let pictures do most of my talking.

Sincerely yours
Claude L Barnes

My father and Mother Frank & Emma Barnes

Grandmother Annie Barnes

This is Tabor, Texas.
In this Building was Housed General Merchandise and the Post Office operated by Mr. T. Branch

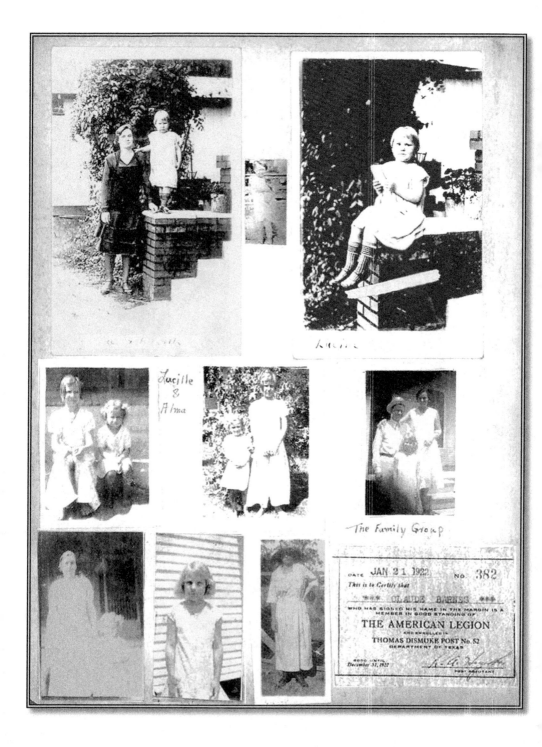

Lucille & Alma

The Family Group

My mother was an only child, named Martha Lucille after her maternal grandmother, born in the Heights neighborhood of Houston in 1922. She was the baby who survived out of three attempts, after one miscarriage and a stillbirth. She grew up in the two-bedroom house my grandfather had ordered in pre-cut and numbered bundles from the Sears and Roebuck's "build-your-own-house" catalogue and built it as a wedding gift for his fifteen-year-old bride, Lucy Mae.

My grandfather's family was a poor family that owned no pretences. His father, Frank, and mother, Emma, lived as basic a life as people lived in that area, in those circumstances, in that era. When my grandfather was born, they didn't allow themselves the luxury of a second name. My grandfather, Claude Barnes, was just Claude. All the children, like their father and his brothers, had one name: Lilly, Verna, Minnie, and Willy.

Only the well-to-do worried about choosing the appropriate number of names and could afford wasting a second name on their children—or, perhaps, those who were less conservatively austere. The wealthier sometimes added two or three extra names, showing their genealogical importance, family traditions, and connections with the past. The poor, uneducated migrant farmers could barely "afford" to plant one name on each child.

> *In Mexico, many of the indigenous migrant workers don't even name their babies until they are two years old because the mortality rate is so high for infants. They make sure the children will likely survive before naming them.*

My grandfather had a desire to learn more, to go to school, but there were chores that had to be taken care of every day of the week. He could only continue in school if he could rise early enough to complete all his chores before heading off to school on an old horse carrying his little brother and sisters joggling on the horse's rump behind him.

It was that determination that gave him the courage to break the cycle of ignorance by attending his first year at Texas A&M before enlisting in the Navy and serving in WWI on the battle ship USS Ohio.

I suspect that it was the drudgery of this dreary life that made my grandfather's mother, Emma, leave the farm, her husband Frank, and their five barefoot, towheaded children. My grandfather was the eldest and the youngest was still toddling when she left.

Back then farm life was difficult. Women didn't live long lives. It wasn't uncommon for a farmer to go through two, three, or even four wives before he finally succumbed. If a woman lived through childbirth, she still had to deal with the daily hardships and grueling work of poverty to survive each day, especially if she was married to a dirt farmer. Working the fields from before sunup to eke out a meager living, one child on your hip and another dragging the sack as everyone picked their share was simply everyday life. You never owned your own property, and you paid a big percentage of everything you earned to someone else.

> *This story has a lot in common with those of the children we care for in Mexico. A number of the children that we have worked with and cared for were abandoned by their mothers when the youngest was only weeks old. How do women who suffer from depression, postpartum depression, abuse, or hopelessness care for four, five, six, or seven little children without some kind of support system or help?*

Emma, my grandfather's mother and my great-grandmother, didn't fare much better by leaving her family and found that moving to the big city of Houston offered nothing for a woman without a husband, education, or money. So Emma took the route that some women who were brave enough or desperate enough to run away during that time took—she became a prostitute on the streets of downtown Houston.

I knew my great-grandmother Emma, and I remember wondering how my grandfather could be so kind to the mother who left him at such a young age, building her a little house on his property in the last decades of her life and then moving her into "my" bedroom when she became bed-ridden in the last years of her life.

Emma was completely blind from syphilis and suffered from terrible sores. My grandmother, Lucy Mae, diligently washed her each day trying to keep the open sores from getting worse and spreading, but it was a miserable illness, and penicillin was not an option at that time.

I remember Emma's cane banging on the floor beside her bed to call for whatever service she wanted. After she tried to hit my grandmother with that same cane, it was replaced by a little dinner bell, which became even more irritating and much easier for her to ring continually.

As a young child I didn't think she was a very nice woman, reminding me of the "gnarly"-looking witches in the children's fairy tales I read. I thought she was just plain mean and had that sickening smell that comes from the sick and the old. My grandmother would bring a wet washcloth for Emma's face and hands before she ate, and each time Emma would hold onto the rag and ask the same question, "Is it a face rag or bottom rag?" I would think, that's a silly question, now, why would my grandmother give her a *bottom* rag to wash her *face* with?

I know my grandfather was embarrassed that his mother died from syphilis, a disease that was common for the sexually promiscuous and those who were in the "profession," although he never said anything or indicated any disapproval or criticism of her. It was my grandmother who quietly shared that bit of information years later. He was too much of a gentleman to show or express that disrespect.

I was only a child when Emma was in her eighties, so I knew her in only one brief window of her life. Even then I wondered what paths she had had to struggle through. The things she must have seen and suffered. How did she feel leaving her small children and then having to lead such an ugly life to survive? Her story was not unique then, nor is it today.

We find that many of the girls who come to the casa hogar and who do not stay long enough to learn new habits and to develop education-ally will many times leave and eventually repeat the same life choices and mistakes as their mothers. Change doesn't happen overnight. There must be enough time plus the right tools and the determination to break that tragic cycle.

One of the girls who came into Casa Hogar Los Angelitos was 13. Her family produced pornography, and her mother was a prostitute. However, by the time little Martha came into the casa hogar, her mother was no longer a prostitute. Her mother was nothing more than a vegetable who could not even feed herself as a result of the drugs and abuse in her life. Some of the family would bring the mother in to see Martha, and Martha would patiently feed her, wiping her face as she drooled out the side of her mouth.

Martha hated to see how her mother was, yet instead of becoming determined to leave that life behind, she felt guilty that she was living free yet her mother was trapped in this empty body. Her family began to pressure her to leave the casa hogar and to live with them to help care for her mother (her mother needed her). The biggest pressure on all of these kids is guilt. The family piles the guilt on top of their little heads until it becomes so heavy that they simply cave in and can't resist any longer.

As a child, or family member, you don't have the right to your own life. It also seems that every child's basic longing is to be wanted by their family and to live with those who have a biological connec-tion, regardless of the circumstances or the treatment.

Sadly, we have no legal authority or any way to keep children if their family comes to get them and if the authorities have given per-mission for them to return to their homes (which is what usually hap-pens). Martha left within one year, and soon was caught up into the world of prostitution. She was beautiful and smart and could have accomplished almost anything she wanted...but she couldn't seem to escape the destiny that her family had shaped for her.

She came back to visit several times after she left and told me that we were the only place where she had felt safe. The last time I saw her and talked to her, she cried as she said, "Nancy, I have seen things so ugly that you would not even believe."

I tried to help her, encourage her to leave that life, to escape, and to begin again. But she couldn't bring herself to leave. I don't know if it was fear of what would happen if she left or the ingrained belief that this was her place in life...except for a brief time, this ugly world was all she had known from the very time she was born and all she would likely ever know.

My grandmother Lucy Mae—Mama Barnes or Aunt Lucy to most people who knew her later in her life—was "Mama" to me. She was born in the area of Sarasota. This was before the Ringling Brothers Circus made it their winter home and before all the "snow birds" from the north discovered the pleasures of the warm white sand beaches. This was before Sarasota became the destination for Yankees who didn't know what a Florida cracker was or how to speak the quaint sounding "Floridian" pitter patter.

Lucy Mae was married to my grandfather Claude. Like my grandfather, she had also been born into humble circumstances.

The story is told that Lucy Mae was born with a 'veil' over her face (or "caul"—now presumed to be the placenta). According to her mother's Native American tradition or folklore, this meant that she was born "special"—with a sixth sense and the gift of healing. Throughout the years that I knew her, these characteristics were obvious in her daily life, and her natural instinct told her how to care for others.

Lucy Mae's father was called "Bone" Hogan. He was a pioneer of early Florida and a "Cracker." He was a tall, big-boned, lanky, red-headed Irishman with an exaggerated handlebar mustache.

The word "Cracker," when referring to a person rather than something served with soup or salad, has carried a variety of negative definitions and innuendos. George C. Clark, in his book, *Early 1800s*

Florida Traveler, described Crackers: "The Crackers came into Florida from the far ends of Georgia and the Carolinas during the Revolutionary War, planted but little corn and made up the deficiency with whortleberries, blackberries and starvations."

In James Denham's book, *The Florida Cracker in the Early 1800's before the Civil War as Seen through Travelers Accounts*, quotes a traveler during those early days, Branch Cabell, in his interesting description of the Florida Cracker:

> They are vagabonds coming to Florida at the middle of the 1700s... an improvident and lawless set of paupers from the frontiers of Virginia, Maryland, the Carolinas, and Georgia, often as bad as, or worse than the Indians. Generally gaunt, pale and leather skinned, they appeared to know neither necessity nor desire, but only silent, joyless, painless existence, which is perfect in its way as a tree or stone. Their improvidence, however, was cheered frequently by drunkenness and fornication; the perpetual presence of their destitution was alleviated by an absence of moral standards and inasmuch as no form of law coerced Crackers, any divergence of opinion could be terminated, quickly and healthfully, with the fist.

The more civilized accepted definition of "Cracker" comes, however, from the gunshot sound of the whip—the crackin' of the whip. The skilled cow hunters (those who went out into the thickets and swamps looking for lost, stolen, or stray cattle that they could round up and bring in) used those whips to herd the cattle, and the people would hear them and say, "Here come the Crackers." Regardless of the accurate origin, the common ground that encompasses the Cracker is that of poverty and an attitude of self-reliance—they were extremely poor but resourceful people, generally from Irish or Scottish heritage.

Bone's family drove the few head of cattle that they had (or had found caught in the heavy thickets) down the Suwanee River from Georgia, looking for a new life and opportunity. They were crackin' their whips to keep the cows together as they walked through the mosquito infested brush and swamps. Many of those early settlers died from malaria, yellow fever, cholera, and "Indian" attacks. The

Above: E. B. "Bone" Hogan and his dogs;
Right: Martha "Mattie" Locklear

Hogans were settlers in Northern Florida in the early 1800s. They
lived through the burning raids of the Civil War from both North and
South. They forged a life alongside the Indians, though they were
burned out more than once by Indians and were known to be part of
the "dish-rag aristocracy" of "Old" Florida, raising cattle, hunting,
doing a little farming, and working the turpentine pine forests.

There were many expressions, public signs, and writings about
the Irish during the 1800s. One sign that could be seen in places looking for labor might read "Blacks and Irish need not apply!" One of the
more colorful "tongue-in-cheek" expressions about the Irish during
the early years of their migration into the wilderness and frontier
areas of America was, "The Irish are moving up socially when they
marry an Indian."

Bone Hogan was moving up socially when he fell in love with and married one of the Indian "half-breed" Locklear girls, 15-year-old Martha, called "Mattie," and they began to have children.

Throughout our work in Mexico with the different indigenous groups as well as those of Mexican descent who live in the U.S., it is obvious that many societies continue to lump certain nationalities and people into incomprehensible and negative groups, especially when they are perceived to be different or a threat of some kind, whether they're Mexican, Indian, Irish, Jewish, Polish, Swedish, Japanese, etc. We forget that we could easily have been part of that group or that our family might have been part of a similar "group" at one time.

The Locklears had migrated down into the northern area of Florida sometime in the late 1700s and early 1800s to escape the persecution of the Native Americans and those who were of color during that time in the Carolinas. They were farmers with mixed blood, and although they considered themselves to be Native American, they realized the danger they faced if they continued to live in the politically volatile area of their homeland.

Throughout the history of mankind the desire for control, gold, and riches has always been a factor in the treatment of indigenous peoples. The white man wanted the gold along the rivers and creeks of Georgia and the Carolinas and had begun the campaign to rid the areas of "Indians" because the Native Americans had "owned" most of the land along the creeks since they arrived. Many of these Native Americans and mixed-blood people were doctors, lawyers, and statesmen and prominent in their community. But they still held the title of "Indian," which could quickly inflame the emotions and hostility of new settlers.

Florida was a new land—a different country—and was part of the Spanish stronghold, which offered land grants to those who would migrate to that area. My great-grandmother Mattie Locklear's parents spoke English, a little Spanish, and the Creek language. They made their living as farmers, fishermen, and any other way that seemed worthwhile.

Bone was quite a colorful man who did a bit of everything to get by. He was a self-proclaimed veterinarian who could set a broken bone better than most doctors and heal animals with his homemade salves and "healing" hands. He was a butcher when he would lead a cow to his favorite hanging tree, stop her under the tree, take out his six gun, shoot her, hang her up, and do his job. He hunted alligators, selling the meat and skins to the local "alligator bar" and other buyers of the day. Bone was a survivor. He adjusted to his circumstances and the times in which he lived. Perhaps some of that resourcefulness was passed down.

There was a funny story told by one of his neighbors who was a young teen during Bone's later years. This neighbor was in his seventies when I talked to him and still lived in the same neighborhood he and Bone shared. He told how Bone called him and his little brother over to help get a gator out of a ditch and culvert area behind his house.

He told them, "I'm goin' into that culvert, under the water. You boys hold tight to my feet as I go in. When I have the gator, I will shake my foot, and the two of you pull like hell until you see me coming out with the gator."

Most of his body was under the water, and when he shook his foot, they starting pulling as hard and fast as they could. Out came Bone holding on to that gator. At the time, Bone was about seventy-eight years old—but the local authorities still called on him as the local gator expert to go in and get a trapped alligator out of a tight spot when no one else could or would.

He also raised hunting dogs and was an "official" hunting guide in Florida's wild back country. Bone was a Marshal for one of the local communities and a member of the Sheriff's posse, wearing a Sheriff's badge on his vest with a six-gun strapped to his waist everywhere he went until the day he died at the age of 84. He owned five acres of land and five cows when his wife, "Mattie" Locklear (my great-grand-mother), ran away to Texas with a Mr. Davis and left Bone with three children, the youngest being my grandmother, Lucy Mae, at the age of almost three years.

My grandmother remembered running, stumbling after the clapboard wagon her mother was leaving in, sobbing "Mama, Mama!" until she could no longer run and the wagon was long gone.

I know that Bone had five acres and five cows when Mattie left, because in the Sarasota newspaper historical archives (happenings of the day), the comment was made, "She said he couldn't support his family, but he had five acres and five cows."

It's hard to know whether it was the loss of their oldest son Johnny or the excessive affection that Bone had for moonshine and Rockin' Rye Whiskey, but for whatever reason, Mattie left for a new life with a new man.

The boys were a little older, but being a very young girl, my grandmother Lucy Mae was raised by her mother's sister, Aunt Sarah Jane, who lived just down the white sandy dirt road from Bone, surrounded by other Locklears in Hogansville. Aunt Sarah Jane was married to Mr. Summerall, who was classified as a mulatto in one of the early Florida censuses. This classification could mean most anything back then because they just didn't know how to classify this group of multiracial people who settled, pioneered, and lived in "old" Florida.

At some point, my grandmother began to communicate with her mother by mail, reestablishing the relationship. When she reached the age of 14, after graduating from the sixth grade, she left the sandy beaches of Florida and headed to Texas to live with her mother and Mr. Davies. Soon after that, she met Claude Barnes, who was to become her husband.

My grandmother, although she obviously loved her father, was openly ashamed of him and the way he lived. "He ain't nothin' but a Florida Cracker," she would say when I asked about him.

He lived in a two-room Cracker-style shack that was more like a shed than a house. He cooked and slept on one side and during bad weather his horse slept on the other side. He skinned rattlesnakes, sold their skins, and ate the meat. The last time she went to visit him in Sarasota, she took him a new set of brown khakis, made a big fire, and burned his old ones. Those had been the ones he wore every day without bothering to change or wash. Then she made him get into the big galvanized wash tub to scrub off the crusted dirt with a bar of homemade lye soap.

I find this man, these people, and this tough and resilient area of America fascinating. However, as I look back from my comfortable surroundings, it is easy to romanticize a time I didn't have to live through and people I didn't have to live with.

Perhaps this little bit of history is important only because both my grandmother and grandfather had been abandoned by their mothers. Perhaps it is important because I find myself in complete comfort around the earthier people and respect those who live off the land but don't always have running water or bathtubs and who have found themselves in a lifestyle without the luxuries that most of us have learned to expect.

Perhaps I have an empathy and acceptance that comes from deep within my bones. Perhaps my family and my past have given me an understanding of difficult times suffered by those I know, those I have seen, and those I am connected to and have loved without ever knowing.

There are so many things about Mexico that remind me of this time and this place. Perhaps that is one reason why I find Mexico so fascinating.

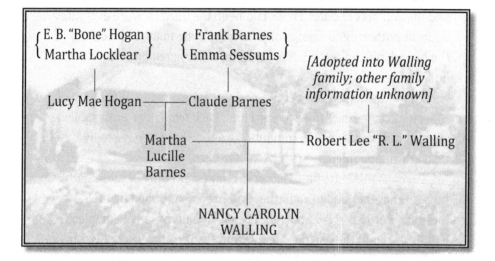

CHAPTER II

My mother, Martha Lucille, married young, at the age of seventeen, before graduating from Reagan High School and had her first child, my older brother, thirteen months later.

Tragedy struck this marriage in the form of viral pneumonia and the new "wonder" drug, sulfa.

World War II had begun, and young men who didn't go into the war began working in areas that were considered important to the safety and security of the "war at home." Brown's tool company was putting out a ship per week. The Houston ship yard was being prepared for the "world at war" and my twenty-two-year-old father began the night shift at the "winter damp," cold, Houston shipyard.

I was six months old when my father "came down" with shipyard, sometimes called "labor" (viral), pneumonia. He was hospitalized just before Christmas, and as his temperature rose, the doctors gave him sulfa. Not realizing or considering that he was allergic to the sulfa, which was causing his temperature to soar, they gave him more sulfa and continued plying him with sulfa until he finally went into convulsions and died, two days after Christmas day.

Robert Lee "R. L." Walling and Martha Lucille Barnes Walling

My father had been adopted into the Walling family. There are no records of his birth or of his adoption. I have spent a great deal of time over the years looking for lost papers or records or something that would tell me a little bit about who he might have been or where he originated. When I was younger and would try to ask my maternal grandmother about my father her comment would be something like "It's best to let sleeping dogs lie."

I have been told by those who knew my father that he was a very handsome young man—outgoing and "never met a stranger." He loved his beautiful wife and babies along with the big "Indian" motorcycle he would spend hours polishing and riding.

As I was growing up, I had an obsession to know the man who was my father. I pictured him in my mind, sometimes talking to him in the night. I would tell him the sadness I felt and cry as I told myself, "If my father were alive, it would be different."

His fate might have been to die anyway. If he had survived the pneumonia and sulfa, he probably would have been drafted into the service as were most young men his age when the U.S. became one of the Allies in WWII. I will never know that, at least not on this side of life. I do know that he was too young to die.

I remember my mother as a young woman and thought she was the most beautiful woman I knew. She married again several years later to a handsome young rancher—Raymond—who was born into a rugged family that had worked its way from Arkansas in the 1800s to settle in the cow country of central Texas. As was the custom back then, she soon became pregnant with her third child.

Raymond's family was notorious throughout the area for being unfriendly to strangers. It was said that you'd better not show up on their property without an invitation or you would be met by a double barreled shotgun.

It might be a clue to their family lifestyle to mention that later in this large family, two of the brothers got into a little disagreement. One brother pulled out a knife and stabbed his brother, and that brother was able to pull out a gun and shoot the brother who stabbed him. Amazingly, although close to death, they both survived and continued as family working the large ranch. It was a tough country and took tough people to survive.

We lived on that ranch for the first year of my mother's marriage. There are scenes and stories that are etched into my memory that, even though I was a young child, still make me shudder today.

Before my younger brother Lynn was born, his father was drafted and quickly shipped out in the desperation of the final years of the war without the benefit of "boot camp" or basic training.

My mother found that continuing to live on the ranch surrounded by "the family" after her husband had shipped out was next to unbearable. So, my pregnant mother, brother, and I moved back to

Houston to the safety and comfort of my grandparents' home. Eight months later, Raymond was shot by a sniper on the Pacific island of Luzon just days before VJ day, leaving my mother a widow again, now with three small children.

During each difficult period, we moved back in with my mother's parents, Mama (Lucy Mae) and Papa (Claude) Barnes, in their two-bedroom house on West 14th. With the three of us moving in and out of my grandparents' house, Papa had closed in part of the porch so that my brother could have his own room in that area. It was a pretty cool room during the heat of the summer, but it got a little cold during the one or two months of winter. So on Saturday mornings my brother would leave his cold porch and crawl in bed with me, telling me adventure stories he made up, or turning on the little electric radio in my room, listening enthralled to the "Green Hornet" and "The Shadow."

I really loved those mornings and looked forward to the tales he could weave, especially the ones about "Porky" the porcupine. My brother and I were a team, at least I thought we were, so it was always aggravating to me when he would act like a boy and team up against me if he didn't want me to tag along. One time, he and his buddies were playing war with a cannon-shaped piece of wood. I kept coming out and sitting on it, just for fun. My brother found a double-edged razor blade somewhere, stuck it into the wood and waited for me to come sit on it. Well, it worked. After the bandaid patched me up, I was furious, but I left them alone. However, he did get into a lot of trouble for that little mean stunt.

Before the women's movement of the 1960s, '70s, and '80s, divorced or widowed women with children were pretty low on the "desirable for wife" list. Yet, my beautiful mother, who remained vivaciously undaunted, married for the third time, to a young man from the same church and neighborhood and who had just returned from the war.

This time, my brother and I heard the "adults" talking about our future, and we heard that her new husband really didn't want to have a ready-made family, especially as old as my brother and I—he was seven, and I was five. My little brother, who was 2 years old, of course would have to stay with his mother, because he was so young.

My older brother pulled me aside, told me his seven-year-old impression of what was going on and gave me his sage advice about what we should say when the inevitable question was asked.

We were given a choice: "Do you want to stay here, where you have been living, where you have your beds and bedrooms, or do you want to live next door?" Being the mature age that we were, and wanting to do the right thing, the decision had already been made to continue to live with our grandparents in the house that had pretty much been our home, with a few exceptions, for most of our short lives. Next door lived my mother, her new husband, and our baby brother.

I grew up thinking this was all very natural, and although the teachers at school seemed a little confused at times because I had one last name, my grandmother another, my mother another, and my little brother another, I thought it was all quite understandable.

In the first few grades at school and church when we were asked to say our names at the beginning of the new period, I would stand up and rattle off all six names that were floating between the two households, proud that I had so many more than everyone else: "My name is Nancy Carolyn Walling Barnes Cobb Pratt" and then confidently sit down.

My days at Love Elementary were not happy memories. I felt ugly next to the cute little, leggy, long-haired blonde and brunette girls, who, even at the young age of eight, nine, and ten knew how to tease and flirt with the boys in class. I saw myself as chubby, with a pasty white body, freckled all over, no eyelashes, and fine, stringy red hair.

I was the Norman Rockwell painting of the little red-headed waif. I think that red-headed children will have a special place in heaven, because so many of them have a difficult time growing up until they can come to peace with the neon sign on top of their forever white and speckled head and learn to use it to their advantage.

I played a lot by myself, with my older brother, and with the neighborhood boys who were part of the "gang." Those days, a neighborhood gang didn't mean the same thing as it does today. A gang was just a group of scraggly kids that played together, tossed rocks into the streets, built clothes pin guns with rubber bands, played "battle," or talked to each other through tin cans with a tight string connecting each end.

Shortly after my mother married her third husband she made an effort to encourage him to accept us. She had gone to the store, and bought him some dress socks. Sitting in the kitchen of my grandmother's house she gave them to me with instructions "Take them over, give them to Dickie and say 'Here's your socks, Daddy'."

What does a five, almost six year old know about things like that? So, enthusiastically, and even a little excited about the possibility of having someone I could call "Daddy" like the other kids, I ran over with the socks. I went into the bedroom, where he was putting away something in the top of his closet. I noticed for the first time how really tall he was. I put the socks on the bed, smiled my sweetest smile, and said, "Here's your socks, Daddy." He turned towards me with one eyebrow cocked, a firm expression on his face, and very matter of factly said, "I'm not your father, and don't ever call me that again."

I felt my neck and face grow hot and my throat constrict. I wanted to crawl under the bed. I didn't know what to say, and so, I said nothing. I slid out of the room as quickly as I could. That was the beginning of a continually uncomfortable and hurtful "love–hate" relationship over the next twenty-five years with my stepfather.

Through those years I developed the very irritating habit of saying "I'm sorry." In the middle of any conversation, under almost all circumstances, my unconscious comment would be, "Oh, I'm sorry." It didn't matter what it was for, or whether "I'm sorry" was appropriate or not. It just became my mantra. I think it might have been some kind of subconscious assumption that I should be sorry, perhaps sorry that I even existed. Perhaps I felt that I was not worth much and consequently needed to continually apologize for everything.

Even though I continued to feel the subtle rejection that seemed to be emphasized with pet names like "pinky puss" and other remarks made to make me feel a little bit like an imbecile, there was a "golden" period of time as I grew into my middle teen years when my stepfather seemed to like and even casually accept me, at least from a distance.

Those were the preaching years. He had become a very popular lay speaker. He began to spend his nights preparing sermons and his weekends preaching. He would step onto a stage in front of hundreds, even thousands of people at some of the largest and most prestigious churches in the United States—First Baptist Church of Dallas, Bellevue Baptist Church of Memphis and so on—preaching with a dynamic style that was his own special talent, evoking emotions and commitments from the audience and moving in a circuit of evangelists and pastors who would all make the Who's Who list of great leaders of the Christian movement of their day.

I remember watching him with pride when he would choke back his tears during the invitation as people would move forward to accept Jesus as their savior or to dedicate their lives to higher service. He had a talent and a charismatic flare that had been honed through his practice as a trial attorney that evoked emotions, whether positive or negative, and no one could be in his presence without responding in some way.

If the church was a local church, I would sometimes sing as part of the special music, just before the message. By that time in my life, with the help of mascara, I was learning how to look somewhat like an attractive young woman. It was during this period that he seemed proud to have me stand beside him as part of his family.

He was probably one of the best speakers I have ever heard.

Those years didn't last nearly long enough.

During that time, my mother had two more children: my youngest brother, Fred (after whom I named my own son), and my sister, Vicki. By the time my sister was born, I was ready to graduate from high school and move on with my life.

It just didn't seem to be my mother's fate to have a lifelong marriage. After twenty-five years of marriage to her third husband, he fell into the affair trap. He had become disappointed with some of the practices of people on that evangelical circuit and seemed to lose his focus, sliding down that slippery slope of disappointment and disillusion.

Not wanting to bear the thought of being alone again she determined to do whatever it took to hang onto the marriage. She humiliated herself, begging him not to leave. "We can work through this; I can forgive; I will do whatever I need to do." She said, "I would crawl on my knees if I had to in order to keep this marriage together." Nothing doing. At the age of fifty, my mother's marriage was broken irreconcilably, this time by divorce rather than death. She was devastated.

Alone again without the ability to earn a living, she took my teenage sister, left her home in Houston, and moved to Colorado, where I was now living as an adult.

I don't know when or how I came to terms with the sense of abandonment and rejection that I had deep inside as I was growing up. As a child, I never fully understood why my brother and I lived with our grandparents, next door to my mother. Yet I accepted this lifestyle as normal and always thought of my mother as if she were an older sister. I never felt the closeness of mother–daughter with her, but I admired, almost worshipped, and loved her from an emotional distance. However, during the years that followed her divorce, we had the opportunity to become good friends and develop a close relationship, which brought a tremendous amount of pleasure and peace into my life.

> *Little did I know that the tenderness and sensitivity about my feelings of abandonment and the pain of rejection—and the longing that I buried deep in my own heart during those early years—would be the very feelings I would need today in working with children who face hurt, deception, rejection, and abandonment.*

CHAPTER III

I grew up "in the Church" in Houston (which is considered part of the infamous Bible Belt) as a Southern Baptist. I literally did grow up in the church. We lived two blocks from West 14th Avenue Baptist, a neighborhood church my grandfather helped to build and my mother attended from the time she was born.

From earliest memory, I seldom missed any service or activity at church, and there were always services and activities—RAs, GAs, YWA, VBS, Sunday School, BTU, WMU, revivals, retreats, Bible studies, prayer band, choir practice, and then, in college, BSU. There were probably many others that I can't recall. As I look back, my "church life" gave me a biblical foundation and was the one place where I felt good about myself.

I knew everyone by name and felt part of a large family where everyone seemed to love and accept me. I remember Naomi, who sat smiling at the desk we all had to pass to go to the elementary Sunday School classes. She always seemed glad to see me, complimented me on something, and had such a sweetness about her. I thought, "I want to be just like her when I grow up."

I became the poster girl for every mother who could say to their out of control teenage girl, "Why can't you be more like Nancy?" I was the "goody two-shoes" girl, as "pure" as the driven snow. I cringe remembering that even today, that was really embarrassing.

I was like a sponge. I loved learning, I loved reading and studying the Bible, I loved the security of knowing that I was saved and that I had a "father" in heaven who knew my heart and loved me.

I "walked down the aisle" to make a public profession of faith at the tender age of eight, and Brother Hollems baptized me one week later in the big baptismal tank that was the focal point at the front of the church just behind the choir.

I climbed up the stairs in my white robe ready to go under the water. I wondered if I would lose my footing, if he would let me fall into the deep water and I would embarrass myself, sputtering or choking, or worse, drowning. I was so afraid of going under water. What if my robe clung to me and people could see my chubby body underneath, or worse yet, my undeveloped breasts?

He held a dry, white, folded-over handkerchief over my nose and pushed me under backwards, "I baptize you in the Name of the Father and the Son and the Holy Ghost." Back then all the preachers used "Holy Ghost" instead of "Holy Spirit." Then it was over, I had been immersed in that big tank of water, and I had survived.

My mother was there, of course. She was at every church service because she was the church organist, the Sunday School principal, and a lot of other things as well. My grandparents, Claude and Lucy Mae, weren't there. They didn't go to church anymore. It had something to do with one of the deacons standing up during a Wednesday night prayer meeting and accusing my grandfather of having an affair with one of the unmarried church women. It was a terrible thing to do to a man like my grandfather.

My grandfather was one of a rare breed of men who would not say a "bad" word any worse than "pshaw" even if he slammed his thumb with a hammer. He would not take a penny that wasn't his or do anything that might look wrong or inappropriate.

When he was younger, the church refused to make Papa a Deacon because he didn't have his wife "under subjection." Mama had been raised in the Pentecostal church and was baptized in that church. She refused to be baptized a second time (into the Baptist church), as was required to become a member, saying, "I don't need to be re-baptized. My baptism was accepted in God's eyes."

> *Although I understand the doctrine behind this denominational regulation, I wonder at times what the first question will be when we arrive in Heaven...will it be, "Which church were you baptized in?" or perhaps, "Now, what denomination were you?" I think it might more likely be, "What did you do to help the poor, the widows, the hungry, the orphans?"*

Papa was the church clerk for many years and was considered one of the pillars of the church. But he never quite recovered from the humiliation and embarrassment of such a public and false accusation. He walked out and never returned.

This background, the love that I had for studying the Bible, the continual involvement in church, and the personal faith that I held in my heart would prove to be the foundation of strength and the centering that carried me through heartbreak, disappointments and challenges through the different stages of my adult life.

Between the age of twelve and sixteen, I rededicated my life at least twice a year. Those were the revival years, the peak of camp meetings, gospel quartets, the big campaigns with evangelists like Freddy Gage, young James Robinson, Billy Graham, J. Harold Smith, and hundreds more.

Southern Baptists believe "once saved always saved," which would prove to be a doctrinal confidence that I would need to hold on to at various times later in my life. However, my dedication and youthful fervor just wouldn't let me sit in my chair when the call was made from the altar to admit publicly that I was a sinner and wanted to rededicate my life.

When I was thirteen I was enthralled with the writings of David, the "Shepherd boy" who became King over Israel. Then, I began reading Proverbs and Ecclesiastes, which, according to tradition was written by David's son Solomon. I read the books over and over.

I found the part when Solomon became King, and "the Lord appeared to him in a dream, and said, 'Ask for whatever you want me to give you'." I would imagine that Solomon thought for at least a minute or two and then answered. "I am only a little child and do not know how to carry out my duties. So, give your servant a discerning heart (wisdom) to govern your people and to distinguish between right and wrong." The Lord was pleased that Solomon had asked for this. So God said to him, "Since you have asked for this and not for long life or wealth for yourself, I will do what you have asked. I will give you a wise and discerning heart." (I Kings 3:7–12 [NIV])

God had granted Solomon his wish because he prayed for what he needed to do his job—wisdom—rather than riches and fame. So like Solomon, who asked for wisdom, I began to pray for wisdom (which I thought would make me wise, like Solomon), and I added one more request asking that God would grant me patience, which I was always short on. I knew in my heart that God had a special purpose for my life, and I wanted to be prepared. I don't know where this confidence came from—certainly not from the encouragement of my family, but somewhere deep inside my soul.

Then at the age of 14, I felt called to missions—China, Africa, India. I was sure about my calling, but I secretly told myself that if I didn't go into the mission field I would probably become a pastor's wife.

Well, that didn't happen. Those guys that were going into some kind of ministry, and there did seem to be a lot of them at that time, just liked the cute, petite, giggly girls. I was far too serious and not very petite. I had grown up into a serious, dedicated, red-headed Amazon.

I remember practicing my music every afternoon at our old upright piano, which was originally a "player" but had been converted when player pianos lost their popularity or their function (too bad some *people* can't be converted when *they* lose their popularity or function). Mama came into the room and stood there for awhile looking at me and then said, "Why can't you just be like other girls?"

"What does that mean?" I thought, "What are other girls like?" I didn't have a clue, nor did I have any idea why she would suddenly say that. Why can't I be like other girls? I don't know.

One of the most difficult things we have to deal with in our challenge to change the lives of the children who come into our care from emotionally and physically difficult circumstances, as well as generational poverty, is to find a way to give these children the tools and opportunity that will enable them to have the confidence to break away from their family and peer group who fight to keep them in the same hole that they are in. The emotional tug is always there: "Why can't you be just like me? Why do you want to be different?" If you move out of the cycle, out of the hole, then you are abandoning your family, friends, and the life that has been created for you and telling them that they aren't good enough for you. The pressure of family guilt can be overwhelming.

There tends to be an unspoken social pressure for children to remain in the same basic standards that they have come from. In India they call it a "caste" system...In Mexico there isn't a name for the "system"—you just do not expect to move much beyond the level you were born in.

In one of the migrant camps in Mexico we were working with a young woman whose little girl had broken her leg, but she didn't realize that until we took her to the doctor, and they were able to put a cast on her leg...she just knew it hurt a lot. This woman was living with her family and about twenty-five other families, all connected in some way. They worked the fields all day, returning to camp in the evening. Camp consisted of a black tarp or black plastic garbage bag, held up by sticks, covering a cardboard bed, a few wooden crates, and some clothes hanging from other sticks in the dirt. She washed her children in a trough; they had almost nothing to eat, and drinking water was taken from the same trough that they washed in.

She was a widow with five little children—none with even the slimmest possibility of ever going to school. We talked to her and offered her the possibility of coming into the casa hogar, helping us with the babies and putting her children into school. She wanted to do that so badly...but she had to ask her family's permission.

The next day when we arrived to talk with her and ask what her decision was, it was obvious by the look on her face that she would say no. She told us that when she asked her father for permission to leave and live in the casa hogar with her children, he was very angry and his reply was, "What's wrong? Am I not providing well enough for you?"

By the time I turned seventeen, I was very active in school—an editor for the school paper, involved in speech, drama, journalism, and music, and played, of all things, first baritone horn in the concert and marching band.

If you aren't familiar with the brass baritone, let me explain, it is almost as large as the big brass *oom-pa-pa* tuba that the big guys carry around. I had to take it home to practice on weekends as part of my music grade. I could barely carry it down the street from the bus stop. It was humiliating walking with the other kids that lived on my dirt road, banging my legs with the case and trying to juggle my school books at the same time.

I wanted to play the flute, clarinet, or, worst case scenario, the French horn. Because I was already taking piano I had to choose a school instrument, and the baritone was the only one left. It was my musical cross to bear. I secretly enjoyed playing, but publicly hated the red ring around my lips from the mouth piece and the masculine feeling I had lugging that big thing around. According to the boys in the band, the lip exercise supposedly made you a good kisser. I wouldn't know about that, at least not at that time in my life.

Finally, I learned how to put on mascara and lipstick and stop my mother from giving me a tight box perm every six months, and I started feeling pretty. That meant I took a new interest in boys, and actually "dated" a few. Well, if you call sitting by your "boyfriend" on the bus to and from school "dating," then I dated a few.

During my high school years at Cy-Fair I was fortunate enough to have two teachers that were really tough on me, but with this toughness they gave me a sense of confidence and made me push for excellence. It's amazing how much influence a teacher can have on a young person. My speech and drama teacher (now called forensics) "Miss Mallot" took me under her wing and gave me—rather pushed me into—the opportunity to develop and learn.

Jewel Gibson, the advisor for the school newspaper and my journalism teacher, was an eccentric and extremely talented journalist whose national claim to fame was a Broadway play starring Burl Ives, called "Black Gold." She believed in me and taught me that I could do anything I set my mind to do. If I could visualize it, I could do it.

It was these two women who gave me the courage to believe that I could make a difference, that I could *be* different.

When I actually started dating an older boy (two years older) and going to the drive-in movie theater on South Shepherd, I found myself looking for an excuse to walk the seven or eight blocks to where he was working every chance I got. I gave up the dream of being a missionary or pastor's wife—none of those guys ever paid any attention to me anyway—and by default I chose a different direction.

One of my least favorite experiences—and one that I didn't learn a thing from except that I never wanted to do that again—happened the summer between my junior and senior year. It was the Ray Duval Funeral home summer. It just happened that my stepfather was related to Ray Duval, and he had made it possible for my brother and me to work that summer to earn some "experience" and extra money. My brother got to ride in the ambulance to pick up dead people, but me, I got stuck at the funeral home all day. Okay, receptionist, organist for funerals, and showing compassion to the grieving family I could handle, but when I was challenged and then enlisted to do the hair and makeup for some of the women—the women on the slab. That experience traumatized me all summer. It felt as if I were watching a horror movie, and I was the star.

It took all my strength not to "freak out" the first time I entered "that" room. I held onto the side of the door and took a deep breath, trying to calm the palpitations of my heart—which had moved up into my throat—and repeated over and over to myself, "She is just a mannequin, she is just a mannequin, mannequin, mannequin," as I walked in and began working on that cold, hard, embalmed, naked body.

I don't know why I agreed to this challenge, whether it was because I always had a hard time saying "No (thanks)" or whether I just would not allow myself to admit my fear. My sixth-grade teacher told me I was obstinate. Maybe that was it.

I'm still trying to figure out what the funeral home lesson was; perhaps knowing that after the family leaves there are personal conversations, jokes, and just a few strange and funny experiences. Even stoic and quiet-talking funeral directors are normal people once everyone else leaves. Perhaps I had this experience to prepare me for another horrible experience I would have to face later in my life as I would stare helplessly at another body laying on a cold slab in the LA morgue. Or perhaps the lesson was that I can do anything—if I have to.

Most of my friends were getting married as soon as they graduated. The others were either pregnant or engaged to be married. So, after graduating from high school, I followed the trend of the time. I made plans to marry the young man I kept walking blocks to hang around. He was smart, funny, and sensitive. We were friends.

During the year before the wedding, I tried to break out of the seriousness of the relationship several times. There were just a lot of other, more exciting boys I wanted to date. But he would cry and seemed so hurt, I couldn't do it.

From the time I was old enough to begin to imagine my future life, my dream was to have my own home, a family, and a husband. I had been collecting items for my "hope" chest for years, and now my dream was about to come true.

My wedding dress was borrowed because we didn't have the money to buy a new one, or, at least, no one was willing to make that purchase for my wedding. At church, a sweet lady friend offered her daughter's dress for me to use and with a few adjustments I found that it fit me perfectly.

I chose autumn colors for the bridesmaids. I guess at the time, I thought those colors would look good on me because of my hair, but what was I thinking? Brown and orange looked a lot like the football corsages that we wore during homecoming, not a romantic wedding.

On the way to the church there was a terrible thunderstorm, lightning crashing in front of our car, thunder cracking loud enough to frighten even the bravest heart, and a drenching Houston monsoon-type rain that slowed traffic down to 30 mph. I had an ominous feeling that I tried to push out of my mind. The thought kept popping up about rain on your wedding day being bad luck; the harder the rain, the harder the luck.

I remember my mother turning to me in the car and saying, "You don't have to go through with this if you don't want to." But how could I back out? All those people were waiting for me at the church. The entire congregation would be there. The church that had made me feel like I had a family, like I belonged, was now a trap. I simply didn't have the courage to back out.

During those years, the announcement would be made in church and the invitation open for everyone. There were no sit-down dinners (unless you came from money, or weren't part of a family church like mine), just a big two- or three-layer cake, mints, punch, and coffee. And maybe little white napkins with the bride and groom's name engraved on them. Naomi made the cake and others helped with the punch and coffee.

My grandparents didn't come—their way of letting me know their disapproval, I suppose. Funny how it was never discussed; I didn't ask, and they didn't say. But somehow we all just knew they wouldn't be there.

I had invited the church janitor, Alex, who happened to be black and was someone I really liked to talk with each time I went to church. Always a big white grin with one tooth trimmed in gold. "How're y'all today, Miz Nancy?"

Of course, he stood at the back of the church, as people would expect him to do during those pre-integration years. Alex was the pastor of his own church in the black area of Houston, and he worked as a janitor at our church in order to provide for his family. I never really thought about him being black or there being a problem with that, but I think he must have thought about it. Actually, I never thought about segregation or the subtleties of maintaining that segregation until I moved away and had the opportunity to experience life differently.

Twelve months later, shaking uncontrollably, my teeth chattering, I poured out my heart to a neighborhood psychologist, feeling close to suicide, depressed, and wondering what was wrong with me. I had been married for one year and my husband—my friend—had never made any sexual or intimate advances toward me. Our marriage had never been consummated and, unlike many of the girls my age—especially the married ones—I was still a virgin.

I had listened against the door of the bathroom, thinking I might hear something that would help me to understand why he wasn't interested in me. I watched him with other people, especially one close male friend he had. I read books about sex and wore what I thought were sexy "nighties," called "baby dolls" back then. I would kiss him and hold him and talk to him, but even at the slightest aggressiveness on my part, he would break out into a cold sweat and turn away. "What is wrong with me?" I asked myself over and over.

We slept in the same bed every night, and I would lay awake in despair, not knowing what to do. I can't answer the question of why I didn't leave right away, except I was terribly inexperienced, and I didn't want to hurt him or have him feel that I was rejecting him—we were friends. I thought perhaps I was the problem, and somehow, with time, I could find a solution to the problem.

I don't think it takes a rocket scientist (although that was the year of the first rocket launch) to figure out what the continual rejection was doing to my already bruised self-esteem.

That year my grandfather, Papa, died of an illness similar to leukemia. His grey-blue eyes that once sparkled with life grew dull and listless, and his hands—hands that had helped build homes and churches, that labored for his family and friends, that planted gardens, and through the years took orphaned children (and sometimes adults) into his home—those hands changed daily, from strong, calloused, and weather-worn hands to a strange and unfamiliar chalky frailty.

I could barely stand to watch, to see the pounding of his heart through his pajamas, and I would emotionally clutch my own heart trying to fight back the tears, wanting to tell him how much we loved him, how much I loved him, but the words never came, and he died.

My grandfather was a good man, but he was not an affectionate man with my brother and me. I think it was the era that he grew up in and the circumstances, but he was never able to hug or touch or express any affection for us. Consequently it was awkward to feel the confidence to tell him how much he was loved or to openly express that love and appreciation to him.

I felt my life was over. I had married against my grandparents' wishes. I had been living a lie during those twelve months, publicly pretending that everything was great, but secretly in so much pain and depression, feeling alone and confused, wanting to do the right thing but not knowing exactly what was wrong or what I should or could do.

Finally, in my desperation, I was able to muster enough courage to make an appointment with a neighborhood psychologist. I needed help, and I didn't feel that I could go to anyone in my family or in the church. I had pretty much kept to myself and didn't have any close friends. I didn't want anyone to know.

It was a shock for me to find out during the first meeting with the psychologist that, by coincidence, he was familiar with the family I had married into and had counseled this young man when he was about fourteen or fifteen years old, several years before I had met him. He had been called in by the family for psychological evaluation as part of a molestation charge against him.

I could hear the words "latent homosexual" and "annulment," but I was shaking so hard I couldn't make my words come out. I couldn't seem to register the words I was hearing. Why didn't someone tell me! How did this happen?

I think my grandfather must have suspected and that was why he was opposed to the marriage, but no one ever indicated that there might be this kind of problem. People just didn't talk about "that."

I thank God for that psychologist; he saw my desperation and humiliation and helped me take the next step. I told him that I couldn't possibly go to my stepfather for help even though he was an attorney. He dialed a friend of his, an attorney, explained the situation, and handed me the phone. Most people never knew the circumstances or why the marriage was annulled. I didn't talk about it.

When his mother insisted on knowing how I could do such a thing to her son, and I tried to explain. She was furious and refused to believe the truth, even though she did acknowledge the problem they had when he was 14, but "they assumed since he started dating me that everything was okay."

It was several weeks after he moved back in with his mother that I had a visitor. It was one of his older brothers, someone I had cared about and that we had socialized with. I was glad to see him because I had always enjoyed the relationship with him and his wife; however, it seemed that he had a different agenda for his visit.

He told me that he had come to find out for himself if "it" was true. In his mind, there was only one way he could prove the truth: He could prove that I was not a "virgin."

Once I realized what was happening, I was petrified with fear and confusion. My legs went weak, and I felt a sick sense of shame and humiliation. Inside my head, I was screaming *NO! NO! NOOOO!* But no sound came out of my mouth. I went into some kind of painful, immobilized trance. I couldn't believe what was happening; it was as if I wasn't there, and I didn't have the strength to resist. I couldn't run, and I couldn't scream or fight back. How could he do this? How could this be happening? He was a friend, family. I was so frightened and hurt....

As I lay curled up in a fetal position of depression, blood on my legs and on the bed, I thought, I can't tell *anyone*. My mind was numb, and I felt desperate; *what can I do!?*

It would be impossible to prove—humiliating, and what would it do to his family, his wife? But what if I am pregnant? I would never be able to have the marriage annulled; what if, *what if*?? The fear and confusion; I felt so shamed and dirty, an overwhelming sense of violation and deception. How could I ever trust anyone again?

Like so much of my life growing up, I felt deep inside that it must be my fault. I needed to be "sorry."

Perhaps it is out of every awful situation that we have the opportunity to learn and grow. That year helped me to see how many people might be living a double life like I lived, and gave me a deeper understanding and compassion for people who suffer in silence while wearing the mask of happiness. The young man I married—how he must have suffered, also living a lie. No one suspected the despair and sense of rejection that I was living with every minute—the horror I was going through—and no one to share it with.

There are so many children and young teen girls and boys who are molested and raped by family members or friends of family over and over. We wonder how they could let that happen, why don't they fight...why don't they run?

Pila cowered in the corner of the one-room house that she lived in with her mother and one of the men who now lived in the house with them. She waited in fear of what she knew was coming...a broken beer bottle thrown at her face or body..."Tonto burra," stupid donkey, he drunkenly yelled at her, swaggering towards her closer and closer. This wasn't the first time. Each time her mother would leave her, sometimes all day and night, alone with this man. She would try to make her little seven-year-old body as small and invisible as possible. But he would seek her out as he became more and more intoxicated, throwing broken bottles at her—or anything else he might have in his hands during his fits of rage.

This time as he moved closer, growling his insults at her, he began to unzip his dirty and worn trousers, glaring at her as she moved into the corner whimpering like a frightened and wounded animal. She tried to protest, but her little voice was frozen in her throat as he pulled her face towards him by her hair and forced himself on her. She couldn't stop crying and whimpering, still in the corner of the dark and dingy room waiting for her mother to return.

It wasn't until the next morning that her mother finally returned to find her little girl still waiting in the corner...her ankle and face with dried blood from the broken glass that had cut her the night before.

She held onto her mother and began to sob as she told her mother of the ordeal of the night before. Her mother—a woman who had long since become mentally unstable from her hard life as a prostitute and the drug abuse that became part of that life—stared at her little girl and then started yelling at her, "Shut up, you are lying!"

Instead of embracing her young daughter and giving her comfort, she began to beat her with her fists. "Don't ever say anything like that again!" During this time of abuse, Pila had become so traumatized that it affected her speech pattern and her emotional development, causing her to develop learning difficulties and emotional instability. It was a neighbor who finally reported the abuse and brought her to the authorities for help and put her into our care.

> *When it happened to me, I was an adult; I had just turned nine-teen years old, and still I couldn't run. I couldn't fight for myself. I didn't know what to do. I felt betrayed, confused, humiliated, and trapped. I couldn't stop what was happening...he was family, a friend. How much more vulnerable, helpless, and confused are the children?*

I was what some might define as inexperienced or "naïve." If you coupled that with the belief I held that the goodness in everyone is only waiting to be found and that the deep-rooted feeling that anything bad that ever happened was somehow my fault, it is easy to see why the first decades of my life were difficult and full of bad choices.

There are descriptive buzzwords that have been coined over the past twenty to thirty years. One of the phrases that seems to fit people who grew up like I did and like the children I see at the casa hogar is "shame based."

Shame-based children grow up believing that it must be *their* fault that their mother abandoned them, that their father abused them, or that they could never prove to be good enough. They lack the inner emotional confidence to believe that they deserve to be treated with respect, deserve to be loved, or deserve the right to make good choices for themselves. Deep inside, they believe they must be unlovable because of the way they look, their personality, attitude, the color of their hair, something, or perhaps even just the fact that they exist.

So, those children either 1) succumb to the idea that they are unlovable, usually becoming "underachievers" who act out the negative behavior that they lay claim to; or 2) they may become overachievers, always trying to do better, look better, behave better, to change, to prove that they are worthwhile and lovable. Somehow, this sense of shame of who they are at the core of their being has to change before they can change—before they can break the downward spiral that they are caught in.

Every child, in order to have a healthy self-esteem, needs to feel that they are accepted and loved for who they are, not out of pity or sympathy or with conditions. My older brother once said, "If your mother doesn't love you, then who can?" When a child feels abandoned and alone, this tape continues to play in their subconscious. If your mother doesn't love you, then who can?

I believe that only God, who knows our hearts, can love unconditionally. However, as parents and caregivers, brothers and sisters, it is our responsibility to do our best to be an example of that type of love. On one of my tables I have a rock where I painted the words, "We like *because*; We love regardless." Children need to feel that they are loved regardless.

Throughout the next fifteen to twenty years, my life was one crisis after the other, tossing back and forth like a ship trying to survive a storm. I am aware that there will be those who shake their heads, or purse their lips and be surprised, feel disappointed, disillusioned, or "put off" by my kaleidoscope of experiences. However, there may be others who cry and say, "If she can live through those abuses, wrestle with her faith, and if God can still use her life, her mistakes, her experiences, the tragedies, the mistakes, if she can overcome, then there's hope for me."

It is for you that I am sharing these things.

I believe that the difficult things that happen to us, the mistakes we make, the combination of experiences that we become victims of, can all be turned into understanding and strength enabling us to use those experiences for a deeper and more productive life. For many years, I saw a yellowed piece of paper that my grandmother put on her refrigerator door: "Life is like a grindstone. It either breaks you to pieces or grinds you into a fine jewel."

King David of the Old Testament grew from humble beginnings, a "shepherd boy" who loved the Lord with all his heart, but as his adult life developed he made some terrible mistakes, including adultery, murder, deception, and theft. Yet, David was used as the leader who brought together the nation of Israel, leading it to a time of greatness. He overcame his mistakes, he prayed with sincerity and repentance that God would "restore unto him the 'joy' of his salvation" and give him the strength to be what he needed to be, and he found God to be faithful.

I have always been fascinated that David was the only "hero" of the Bible that I have found to be referred to in the New Testament as "a man after God's own heart." Wow—a liar, adulterer, murderer, and thief, called "a man after God's own heart." David is a good example for all of us who have made mistakes and felt that the "dirtiness" of our lives made us unworthy to be of use for God's work. I believe God sees our hearts differently than the world sees us. David loved God and longed for a close relationship with Him. Perhaps it was the love that God saw through all the humanness that made him special.

After going through an annulment of my marriage, I wanted to enroll at Sam Houston State College (at that time it was a college; now, it's a large university) because they had offered me a scholarship while I was in high school, and I wanted to try to pick up where I had left off.

During the previous year and half I had been working while studying at the Houston Conservatory of Music but felt I wanted to return to full time study. I wanted to be a teacher.

I went to the registrar's office to talk about scholarships and enrollment and I was terribly disappointed when I was told that a scholarship and financial aid was no longer possible for me, and that if I enrolled in school I would have to live in the apartments (which were more expensive) with the older students. I would not be able to stay in the dorms because I had been married and might be a bad influence or example for the other girls.

I think there are definitely times when I should have learned to shut my mouth and not assume that everyone would accept my situation with open arms and compassionate understanding. This was one of those times.

I struggled for several years, working parttime during the week and driving the seventy-five miles home each weekend to teach piano students in order to pay my expenses and continue my education. But it was just too financially difficult at the time. My brother was finishing his education at the University of Corpus Christi and had been able to get financial aid as well as some extra help from family, but that had not been available for me, so I had to drop out.

Guilt is the gift of shame that keeps on giving...Grace is God's gift that defeats guilt and shame...Faith gives us the strength to accept that grace... and Hope to look for the future.

Unknown

Therefore, since we have been justified through faith, we have peace with God through our Lord Jesus Christ, through whom we have gained access by faith into this grace in which we now stand. And we rejoice in the hope of the glory of God Not only so, but we also rejoice in our sufferings, because we know that suffering produces perseverance; perseverance, character; and character, hope. And hope does not put us to shame, because God's love has been poured out into our hearts through the Holy Spirit, who has been given to us.

Romans 5:1–5 (NIV)

CHAPTER IV

I felt that I was floundering without a plan or a future, and that's when I met Albert. I didn't like him much when I first met him, but he was persistent and obviously very interested in me. After spending more than a year in a relationship with a person who wasn't interested in me at all, I found myself attracted to his aggressive, although slightly obnoxious, approach.

Once again my family didn't approve of my relationship, so, with my new love's encouragement, we ran away, in my car, to Dallas, to the justice of peace, and "got" married.

What a shock for me the first night of our marriage when Albert shared some of his past with me. He had been married before; he had a child and had been thrown in prison by his first wife's family in order to have the marriage annulled. But sad to say, that deception was only the beginning of all the deception that became like a black, unending nightmare for me.

I had given Albert postcards to mail to my family telling them that I was married and living in Dallas. I found out later that those postcards were never mailed and that my family was desperately looking for me. I didn't realize at the time that *he* didn't want anyone to know where *he* was.

I began to realize even more when I received a call through our landlord from my family back in Houston. They had found my location when the bank sent a "collector" to pick up my car in the middle of the night. That morning I woke up to find my car gone. I thought it had been stolen and had no idea that my husband, who had agreed to make the payments on the car for the two months previous, had not only avoided making those payments but was also being hunted by the company that he had previously worked for.

When the payments weren't made, the bank where I had my car loan and had also worked for a time called my family and did their research, finding a long list of questionable concerns related to my new husband and causing them to decide to go after the car and bring it back immediately.

"You need to come home," I heard them say on the other end of the phone as they began to tell me all the things they had found out. I felt as if the blood was draining from my body, and I felt the nausea creeping into my stomach. But I had made a commitment, so I slowly and fearfully said, "I can't; I have to try and help him."

I soon found out I was pregnant, without funds for food or medical attention and had no vehicle to drive—and I was daily discovering more deception.

Deception should be a four-letter word, because it definitely evokes some powerful four-letter words: fear, pain, hate.

The nights that I waited sitting alone in the dark until the early hours of the morning, wondering *Where could he be?*

Of all the things that I left at home when I went to Dallas, my Bible wasn't one of them, so I took out my Bible and read over and over

> ...whatsoever things are true, whatsoever things are honest, whatsoever things are just, whatsoever things are pure, whatsoever things are lovely, whatsoever things are of good report; if there be any praise, think on these things...
>
> Philippians 4:4-8

I held tight to that verse and would make myself think positive thoughts when I felt myself falling into depression or fear. "Whatever is good, think about those things." I took this very literally during those years.

I suffered times of depression since I was a young teen and found myself having to use every bit of my inner strength during this time not to give in to a total collapse into that blackness. I became fearful of everything. Listening in the night for strange sounds, watching my husband sit in the darkness until the early hours of the morning. It was the strangest thing, this feeling that everything was an unknown, nothing was secure; I was living in some kind of a nightmare fog and couldn't see my way out.

I realized how distrustful and frightened I had become when Albert suggested that we go for a romantic boat ride on one of the large lakes in Dallas. It was almost 10 P.M., I was pregnant, and I didn't know how to swim.

I still can't be sure if his suggestion was truly an innocent and potentially romantic one or if, in his desperation, he had another, darker, thought in mind. Regardless, I didn't go, but I wanted to give him the benefit of the doubt. However, I became very aware and guarded against everything that might be a potentially dangerous or vulnerable situation.

We moved from rental to rental every two months, saving the second month's rent while avoiding the past from catching up.

There were always the promises of possible work, leaving the house with briefcase in hand and going "somewhere"—but never a paycheck coming in. When the job I had in downtown Dallas had to be given up because of my advancing pregnancy, I didn't know how we would continue to survive, or at least, how *I* would continue to survive.

We still didn't have a car, so I took a bus to work every morning, and many days I would walk the eight miles home because I didn't have enough money to buy a bus ticket. At the office, I joked about not eating lunch (picking up the packaged saltine crackers or table bread and adding a little catsup or butter on top) and walking home, "trying to stay in good shape and lose a little weight."

Albert would come to the office and pick up my check in front of other people, knowing that I would be too embarrassed to make a scene. He discovered that he could continue to do that throughout our marriage, giving me a small "stipend." I have no idea how my money was spent. What an idiot I was.

Our cupboards were bare most of the time, and I was concerned as I was growing bigger and bigger with my pregnancy. I knew that I had RH negative blood, but I didn't have the money to go to the doctor, and I knew that the hospital required a $50 deposit to go in for delivery. I didn't know what to do.

Finally, Albert found a little apartment advertised in the paper where we could stay for free if we did the management. Now that I was no longer working, the only food we had he bought with hot checks written to Safeway. It was in this position that I had gone into the kitchen to look for something to eat and saw that I had some flour in the cupboard and two pieces of white bread, the heel and the piece next to it. I had planned to make flour gravy and eat those two pieces of bread, when the young woman who lived in the apartment above us knocked on the door, begging.

She was a scraggly looking teenager with dark hair that looked like it hadn't been washed in awhile and a small baby in her arms. Her teeth looked like they had never had much care, and I could hear her baby crying most of the day. She told me that her husband would be home soon, and she didn't have any bread to serve him with his dinner, and he would be so angry with her if she didn't have bread for him. "Could you please loan me some bread?"

I swallowed hard and told her, "I only have a heel and one other piece of bread."

"That will be okay," she said. So I went reluctantly into the kitchen and got the last two pieces of bread and gave them to her.

I decided that's it, I can't go on like this. I can't take a chance on hurting my unborn baby.

I walked the four blocks down to a local diner and pathetically asked the owner if he would lend me a dime so that I could place a collect call to my family on the pay phone he had there. I assured him that the dime would be returned as soon as they accepted my call. Or, if they weren't home or didn't accept the call, the dime would be returned. Either way he would get his dime back.

At first, I didn't think he was going to give me the money. He stood there for a few minutes looking at me, and then I guess he decided to take a chance and said okay. He went to the cash register, took out a dime, and I said a prayer as I dialed the number. The call was accepted. I swallowed my pride and began, "I need to come home. I have lived a terrible life here. I am starving and pregnant and can't even get medical help if I need it. Can you help me? Can you please come for me?"

I planned to leave the next day during the evening when I knew that Albert would be gone. I would have to pack quickly and be gone before he returned. I felt like a thief leaving in the night, but I didn't know how else to get home and find help.

I remember the chicken fried steak that I ate so ravenously when we stopped midway on the trip between Dallas and Houston, and I also remember the nausea and retching as I vomited that chicken fried steak in the bathroom at the back of the restaurant. It had been so long since I had eaten solid food my stomach didn't know how to react.

I celebrated my twenty-first birthday back in Houston, pregnant and not knowing what the future might hold.

My baby was born several months later, and I soon found a job at a neighborhood hardware store in Houston, living again with my grandmother who helped me find an old '56 Buick that I could drive back and forth to work.

I couldn't even think about a divorce, and besides, I had no idea where Albert was living in order to send papers to him.

I was asked to help out a small church that needed an organist and was happy to be going to a new church and feeling productive again.

Of course, the pastor of the church wanted to know why I had a baby and no husband. It was about that time I started getting phone calls from Albert. He had hitchhiked back to Nebraska, where his family lived, after reading an ad that his mother had put into the Dallas paper about the death of his father. Knowing that he read the daily papers obsessively and his last known location was in the Dallas area, she hoped to find him this way.

Once he returned, his family wanted to know where his new wife and baby were. To save face, he made up some story, and he began his campaign to get me to join him in Nebraska.

So, I went to the pastor of this little church where I was going and explained some of the story, as well as my dilemma about going back to this man, and especially to Nebraska, which seemed like a foreign country to me, taking me even further away from my home and family.

"Your place is with your husband; it is your Christian duty," he said, in a matter-of-fact, confident tone. I was sick with the thought. Now what? According to the pastor, the command was clear. According to my family, it was a ridiculous thought. According to my boss, I would go have more children and still end up divorced—don't do it!

As seemed to be my pattern, I ignored all warnings and went to Nebraska, intending to hold on to enough money to buy a plane ticket back home. That never happened, of course, and the money was quickly spent. Within a few months after I arrived, Albert had again quit his job, and once again we had to move in with family. This time it was his family. I had put myself into another trap that I didn't feel I could escape from.

We went from one difficult situation to another, eventually moving to Colorado, where he had a close friend and where he was finally able to get a job that he liked—working as a fireman.

During the first five to six years of our marriage, I counted twenty-one moves in total—and two more children. Some moves were for better, some for worse; none very good. One of the houses was a little one-bedroom cabin at the south end of Horsetooth Reservoir. It didn't have running water or electricity, so with a one-and-a-half-year-old baby and pregnant with my second, I learned how to wash out dirty diapers in a bucket of water, use an ice chest to keep food from spoiling, and thank God for a friend who lived down the hill and let me use her bathroom to take a bath once a week.

I find it funny now to think that I continued to attend church, this time at Northside Southern Baptist Church. I became a Sunday School teacher for teens, which I loved, and I developed a close connection with all of those kids. I maintained a connection with them throughout the years, some even to this day. They gave me energy. They taught me to laugh again and kept me up on the songs of the sixties. I was their teacher, and they were my joy.

The physical hardships were not as much of a problem for me as the continual deception, the lies, and the verbal, emotional, and mental abuse. Friends would get up and move away from us because they couldn't stand to hear the way Albert openly insulted me. It was the kind of verbal manipulation that keeps a person under an emotional bondage and always thinking, "It must be my fault; I must not be worth more; I must deserve to be treated like this." How many spouses continue to stay in a relationship that demeans them because they aren't sure whether they deserve better or are even afraid that a change might be for the worse?

During those years I held at least five different jobs, always looking for a better position. A man that I worked with at a local music store talked me into helping him open a music conservatory in Fort Collins. We opened the Musical Arts Conservatory, and we eventually had twenty-four teachers working through us. This man had severe financial difficulties, so he took his family and left town, and I was left holding the bag. I invited another man who was at that time a professor of music at Colorado State University and was teaching piano for the Conservatory to take over this role: Robert Williams, III, pianist and teacher, who became a dear friend and is still a dear friend some forty years later.

We needed money so Albert put in a bid to do a star mail route out of Loveland. He got the bid, but what I didn't know was that he had intended that I take the full responsibility of the route. It was like a nightmare six days a week. Crawling out of bed before 4 A.M., gathering up my sleeping children, one baby in diapers and still on the bottle, the other two toddlers, not yet in preschool; then driving the eight miles or so to LaPorte so that another lady with four children of her own could receive mine in the middle of the night. Then I would turn around and drive the fifteen dark miles to the Loveland post office to sort and deliver mail up the Thompson Canyon. I had to have all the mail sorted and be out the door on my route by 7 A.M.

I was the first woman to work at the Loveland post office since WWII, and some of the men didn't accept or appreciate my presence there, letting me know right off that I would have to carry my weight because they would not help me, period. I was determined, in my obstinate way, and never asked for help. Sometimes struggling with the loads, but head down and tight-lipped, I did what I thought I had to do. The attitudes did change over that year, many of the men softening and becoming friends.

Some mornings as I would leave the house my left eye felt like raw sandpaper as the abrupt early hour awakening would tear off those delicate dry eye cells. I would drive holding a cold, wet cloth over my eye until the pain finally subsided.

There were days on the road that I came close to death, falling asleep from the fumes and heat off the engine of the car and lack of sleep as I drove from mail box to mail box, driving off the road or into a ditch.

In the evenings I went to the Conservatory to teach piano and do the book work for the other teachers who were working there.

Sometimes by the time I was able to pick up my children and get home, I was so exhausted I really didn't know how I was going to get through the night.

I remember one night pleading with Albert, my face buried against his turned back with tears running down, "Please don't make me go."

Only by the grace of God and the strength I must have pulled from all of those determined people who were part of my past did I survive those days.

Today, I wonder what was wrong with me that I would take a responsibility that someone else put on me and carry it to the point of exhaustion. Why didn't I just say no? I wonder how many other women, and men, find themselves in this kind of trap, feeling like an animal that can't escape without chewing off their own leg. Afraid of whatever unknown is out there.

Now, I know that no one can *make* you do something you really don't want to do. But back then, I was trying to be the good, obedient, Christian wife, fitting what I believed was the right image, trying to find and live the dream—the dream that had for me become a nightmare.

Even then I realized that this was not how God intended marriage to be but thought, "This must be what I deserve since it was my own bad choices that put me in this mess. I must do what I have to do to do the right thing." I really don't know where that "right" thing came from, but somehow I had to find a way to meet my sense of integrity and not throw myself under the bus in order to do it.

I realized that Albert's repeated suggestions that I visit the Colorado mental health facility in Pueblo for a much needed "rest" were intended to break down my confidence and cause me as well as others to question my mental stability. I finally accepted the reality that if I were going to survive and be able to take care of my children, I had to find the courage to make a complete break from this relationship.

After seven very emotionally brutal years of marriage, I took legal action to seek a divorce. It wasn't easy. A very angry, rejected Albert made sure to sadly pass varying negative insinuations, depending on the audience and their connection to me.

Those insinuations painted me in conflict with myself. To one person, he might imply I was a lesbian; to another, I was a prostitute; for my mother, I was an alcoholic (which is one of the worst things for a good Baptist girl)—and I didn't even drink.

None of those things were true, yet the list continued to grow. The scars, pains, and fears within each of us can become easy targets for those who want to manipulate and control in order to meet their own agenda and needs. I was becoming so angry. I felt that I had sacrificed seven years of my life trying to help this person, living in the abuse I lived in, just to find myself being crucified by the very person I tried to help. Where were my boundaries? Where was the justice in all of this? Was I going to just let this happen to me, or was I going to gather my inner strength and stand strong?

A few members of the church that I had been so active in and who surely must have recognized the abusive treatment and difficulty of the relationship turned against me, sucking in the negative waves that always seem to surround something like this.

"How could someone like Nancy change to become what she has become?" And just what might it be that I had "become"? I was simply a woman with three children who finally decided not to live in abuse any longer.

I struggled every day trying to feed my children and provide for them without financial help from their father, my family, or any other source. I understand how it takes a lot of courage for a woman to make a decision like this and then to survive that decision—and even more so during those years *before* women could borrow money on their own, get a job that paid anywhere close to what a man could make, and were automatically considered "loose" if they were divorced.

Most of us have made bad choices, "mistakes"; some more than others. I fall into the latter category. Most of us have regrets and sorrows as a result of those choices. But those paths from the past led us to where we are now. Every road, difficult or easy, brings us to the place we are. It brings us our loves, our children, our friends, our lessons, our locations, and sometimes our wisdom (remember, I prayed for wisdom; we do need to be careful what we pray for).

CHAPTER V

*Each year of life is categorized by the main events...or perhaps even
some small event, but nonetheless years are remembered by events.
1971 is etched in my memory as the year of accidents, heartbreak,
sorrow, and accomplishments...a year of turning and changing. A
year filled with new people and experiences. A year of painful correc-
tion, hope and excitement...all the possibilities of closeness and ful-
fillment, then shattered before time could bring them about.*

*I became an old woman, with sadness wrinkling my eyes, and my
mouth drawn with so many frowns. I find myself recalling the days of
my youth so frequently, as if I were in the twilight of my years, with
no future remaining...*

Nancy

After a very bitter and destructive divorce, I managed a women's
clothing store and then decided that the only way I could get
ahead and have some level of control over my financial future was to
open my own business. So I did. I worked hard and became somewhat successful...and I loved having my freedom.

I felt as if I had been given a tank of oxygen and was finally able to breathe again. I bought a ten-speed bicycle and made friends with other young adults. Riding down the wide streets of Ft. Collins in the cool of the late evening was the most exhilarating thing I had done in a very long time. Nineteen seventy-two became the beginning of freedom, the beginning of new experiences. I bought a vintage 1942 Willys topless Jeep I named "Herbie," and my three children and I would take Herbie to the dirt roads at Horsetooth Reservoir or Rist Canyon or anywhere our hearts desired. Freedom! A time of touching, of doing, of more change —a kaleidoscope of feelings and new hope.

It was the joy of such simple things: traveling down streets, alleys, and parking lots in groups of four, three, two, one. Peddling with the new vitality of youth and freedom, fast, slow, seeing life that I didn't have time to see before.

It was during that time that my heartbroken mother and my teen age sister had come to live with me, and we needed to find a way to increase the income so that two families could be supported, so I decided that if one store worked well, a second would help provide the income to support two families and to make things better. I now know that more is not always better.

Five years later, after numerous competing stores and malls began opening, I found that I didn't have the financial strength to compete or to support two families. I was forced into bankruptcy.

During this time I wrote in my journal.

It has been a long season of depression. I think I hit my low last week. But I can feel myself pulling out. I find myself looking forward to the morning again and wanting to get out of bed to face the day.

Today, 1975, I sat in a room full of people waiting my turn to face the bankruptcy court. A room full of lives depicting financial and personal tragedies, failures...

I remember what I was told when I was so deep in depression... "You face, in your mind, the worse things that can happen. Accept them and then anything less is a step back up." I had faced bankruptcy over a year ago in my mind and now, today, it all seemed so strange, so simple. I almost laughed out loud to think "how so many months of work and torture, worry and frustration could be washed away in five minutes of ambiguous questioning."

I felt two basic feelings: the guilt of being part of a society that takes cover behind protective laws to unload financial debts and re-sponsibilities; and the hope that now I had unshackled my bonds so that I could become a productive part of society again.

I learned so much in these crowded years. Shelby, my attorney, must have seen my need for reassurance or inspiration. He broke into an impromptu elaboration of his philosophy for success.

The people who are really successful in life seem to have two main ingredients. One, faith, faith in life, in themselves and in the concept that things will work out to good. Two, the fortitude to keep trying even against insurmountable odds.

Nancy, 1975

I had been smart enough to file a homestead claim on the house I owned or I would have been without a place to live, without income or transportation, and with three children to feed and care for. It was during the depression of bankruptcy, after losing everything, that I met a young man who had a small daughter. His name was Bob. My mother and her new friend Paul had insisted that I get out of the house and away from my depression and accompany them to a "fun" place in Severance called Bruce's Bar. I reluctantly went, but my first time out of the house for almost a month brought me face to face with this handsome young man who asked me to dance. The relation-ship was on high speed and sealed when he bought me an old station wagon so I had transportation—and then moved in with me. He helped me buy groceries, pay utilities, and kept me from going totally under.

He was a butcher working the line at the nearby Monfort packing company, saving every penny he made and working long hard hours at this physically demanding work.

This relationship continued for more than a year until he decided to move to Laramie and purchase a slaughterhouse and meat-packing plant. I had been working several temporary jobs, and the decision to move was made together, but I told Bob I was not moving to Laramie unless we were married. So, once again, the "woman at the well" had absolutely nothing on me. I am sure that Jesus saw to it that her story was in the Bible just for my benefit.

At the risk of sounding like a continual whiner, from my perspective it was not an easy situation. We worked like dogs, living next to the fairgrounds and in a neighborhood that was considered to be the worst part of town. But that's where the property, the slaughterhouse, was and where we lived. The work was very heavy, physical and not conducive to positive thinking. Killing animals all day, cutting them up, listening to people complain, accusing you of stealing their meat, and then all the lifting, hauling, and cleaning just became overwhelming. This work experience was right up there with—and surpassed—the funeral home.

After my youngest child was born (with my husband's daughter now giving me five children), I just couldn't continue facing the seventy-pound baskets of frozen meat, the freezing lockers, and the continual handling of raw meat, so I decided to give up my partnership in the meat-packing business and go into real estate. As my work became more successful, Bob's business became more difficult, and he began to become more and more depressed. We sold the locker plant, but he continued with the slaughterhouse, killing animals.

I think his sensitivity and depression began to overwhelm his thinking. He went to counseling a few times at my insistence but didn't want to continue paying for that. The medicines were expensive, and he just thought it wasn't worth it. However, the degree of depression and the physical and psychological distress of the work that he was doing seemed to engulf him. One morning in the wee hours, he left the house with the rifle that he used to kill cattle, parked in front of the sheriff's department, put the barrel in his mouth and pulled the trigger.

There's little point in trying to tell how devastating that was for me or how horribly some of his family, as well as others in the community, treated me. There is always blame, and the spouse is first in line. I was well equipped to accept any amount of blame anyone cared to pile on me; I had trained for it my whole life. It is an understatement to say that my determination to keep going and my self-esteem were smashed. I avoided public places. I became dysfunctional and had terrible nightmares about hell.

How can we truly regret those decisions that brought us to where we are now? If I had not gone through the hurts and disappointments that I went through, the challenge of overcoming, how could I have had the courage to do what I am doing now or the perseverance and faith to know that through it all God is still there?

How could I understand so deeply how mothers who are forced to abandoned their children feel, or who think they have no other choice but to go into prostitution to survive, or the shame a child feels being abandoned, abused, rejected, or part of a terribly broken family? In my life or in my family, we have seen or experienced nearly every type of situation.

Could we walk through what we are walking through, and what lies ahead, if we had not walked through what we have walked through?

If there was a section of my life that I could just erase it would have been from those twenty years. However, the beauty that came out of those years include my children, my determination, perseverance, and faith that God loves me, and His Grace is sufficient even in the depths of my sin and imperfection. I went from poster girl to the lowest rung possible.

❦

PART TWO

Speak up for those who cannot speak for themselves, ensure justice for those who are perishing. Yes, speak up for the poor and helpless, and see that they get justice.

Proverbs 8-9 (NLT)

CHAPTER VI

Finally, I had repeated the same mistakes often enough that I began to learn from those mistakes. Perhaps God decided to help me out of my own blundering and brought someone into my life who could love me and care for me...a hero who rescued me from what felt like the depths of hell. I always seemed to be looking for that hero. But this time I wasn't looking. I had given up hope.

Dave was a divorced man with three grown children, and I...well, I was everything and had been through everything—a broken woman with five children...

When I first met Dave Nystrom, there was something about him that reminded me of my grandfather; perhaps the quiet stability and nobility, or the way his knees looked when he was driving the car, or the way he held his hands. I don't know what it was, but for the first time in my life, I felt as if I were being held in the arms of security and protection.

In the same year we married and began our life together, we decided to buy a second home in a Mexican beach town called Manzanillo.

Dave was a successful businessman, and we were both busy with life—working, traveling, moving ahead, raising our eight children, his three and my five. Now don't get me wrong, it wasn't and still isn't all peaches and cream. We were and are two very different people. I am emotional, creative, and visionary. He is practical and able to separate from his emotions with a solid business approach to most everything. Yet if we celebrate the strengths and weaknesses of each other's differences, we complement each other and form a more complete whole. If we were to try to mold the other to be just like we are, then we would have a disaster.

When you blend two families and two strong-minded people, there are problems to overcome and compromises that have to be made. I knew from the beginning that it was impossible for this relationship to work if I couldn't learn to trust again.

Trust is not necessarily an easy instinct to regain once you've lost it. We are born trusting our caregivers completely. However, that trust can be eroded quickly and early in life if our caretaker, family, or those in a position of trust abuse that trust. If parents don't protect a child—if they abandon, abuse, or neglect that child—he soon learns not to trust. If our relationships become abusive or neglectful as adults, we also can learn *not* to trust.

It was hard for me to make a conscious decision to trust again, to trust Dave to be the man I hoped I was marrying, to expose my emotions and intimate self to him. But I made that choice. We both worked hard to make it work. I was not going to fail again.

CHAPTER VII

A journey of faith, spiritual battles, miracles...Death is not the end...

Some memories are engraved in our brains, the first time we meet someone, the first time we see our newborn baby's face, and the last days or hours we spend with someone we love.

It was midnight, and like all the other nights, I could hear the waves from our upstairs bedroom in "Casa Serena." I slide quietly out of bed and wandered over to the sliding glass door that opens onto the upper deck, like every mother from the beginning of time, wondering if my child is home and safe.

Looking out over the bougainvilleas that hung around the edge of the deck and across the bay at the lights of downtown Manzanillo, I saw him, and I sighed with relief. "He's home." There he was sitting on the sea wall, facing the darkness of the night, mesmerized by the sounds of the waves slapping against the sand his legs and feet dangling over the edge, he seemed to be staring at the movement of the water, with each movement the reflection of the moon shimmering against the flecks of "fools gold" that layered the beach. I watched him for awhile, the silhouette now embedded in my memory, then turned around to go back to bed, thinking, "He's home; he's safe."

I don't know how he had even made it to Guadalajara; he got up late, had to drive to the LA airport during heavy traffic, and in his hurry, he lost his ticket while walking from the parking lot to the ticket counter.

Once he discovered that he didn't have his ticket, and the agent said, "Sorry, no ticket—no flight," he ran back toward his car, retracing his steps, looking from side to side at the muddy mess that was there from the recent rain—and there it was, flapping in the breeze, half covered with mud, waving like a flag: "Here I am, here I am!"

Freddy was proud of that near miss. "Mom, I am just the luckiest person. Who would have thought that ticket would be there waiting for me to find it?" This was a special trip for Freddy; he hadn't been to Manzanillo in awhile, a place he loved and where he had spent weeks every year for the past 12 years with us. His new wife, who was a beautiful second-generation Mexican–American, wasn't interested in coming on this trip, so Freddy made the decision to come anyway, alone, on what would prove to be his last trip.

Freddy was born special. When the nurse brought him to me that first time I looked at him, the perfectly shaped red cap of hair that crowned his head, his little pink lips and the white, white complexion that seemed to have a slightly yellow tint, and I thought, "They've made a mistake; this can't be my baby." He didn't look anything like his older brother Eric who was born with a beautiful light olive complexion, big brown eyes, and dark hair. My mother saw my surprise and said, "He will be very special for you."

When Freddy was still just weeks old and we would go to the grocery store, both boys in the shopping cart, two-year-old Eric would attract someone's attention, point, and say, "Look at my little brother; he has red hair."

Even as a child, Freddy had a wide-eyed, enthusiastic look, a sprinkling of freckles on his face, and a wiry little body that was always moving. It was easy to spot him in a crowd even a block away because of his animation and the brilliance of his hair. Freddy did live life to the fullest from the very moment he was born.

I looked at him, the young man who was no longer a child, who seemed so full of life, so full of energy, taking on every challenge—yet I had this anxiety, this gnawing fear that he would do something or try something that would be too dangerous or something that he couldn't control. This was the child I always worried about. "Oh, Freddy," my heart would cringe, "be careful."

The day before he left, Freddy walked up from the beach onto the grassy area below our deck, holding his flippers in one hand and goggles in the other, smiling as he looked up to where I was standing. "Hi, Mommy." He was 28, but he still called me Mommy when he wanted to charm me.

"How was the water?" I asked him.

As he stood there, I'll never forget the way he looked in that moment, his red hair askew, the hairs on his bare chest competing with the red of the sunburn he was starting to get. "Great!" was his typically enthusiastic response.

Freddy, early twenties

As I looked down, a flash went through my mind and heart, and instead of seeing my son, Freddy, I saw my father—my father as I "remembered" him from a photo, standing with the same stance and look, and a cold fear swept through me. My father died when he was 23 years old, a handsome young man with so much life ahead of him. People said he was one of the nicest guys they knew, one who never met a stranger. I grew up studying the few photos that I had of him. I looked at them so often I felt I knew everything about him.

I looked at Freddy and automatically shook my head to shake out the unwelcome thought. "No!" I desperately scolded myself. "Nooo!" I tried to shake the thought, but it was so powerful I couldn't.

Freddy slept on the sofa for the first several days after he arrived in Manzanillo, because our house had filled up with people—friends of my mother and friends of ours, all converging at the same time. How does this happen? A missionary family from deep within Mexico came to visit a pastor friend of ours from Texas. How we became the central collecting point, I don't know. How I wish now that I hadn't worried about entertaining all the "company" but had taken the time and spent every precious minute with my son. If I could only rewind the time.

Seven months later, we were back in Colorado. Dave and I had just finished lunch, and we drove from the restaurant in Eagle heading toward a new housing development that my mother and her husband Paul were interested in looking at. As we were driving, an excruciatingly sharp pain shot through the base of my head. I cried out, grabbing my head in pain. Feeling as if everything was twirling around me in circles, I said, "Dave, please, we have to get out of here! Something is wrong!" It was about 1:30 P.M. Colorado time. I waited in the car, distressed, my head swirling, until they had a chance to go through the houses, then we turned around to head up to Leadville to meet my brother for dinner.

It was almost 7 P.M. when a call came into my brother's house for me. It was my oldest son Eric. Strange for him to call me at my brother's house. He was sobbing and couldn't speak very coherently. "Mom, he didn't mean it. Mom, he didn't mean it."

"Mean what, Eric? Who?"

I was panicked. I thought my daughter's husband might have done something to her because of their separation and pending divorce. My voice began to constrict, and I carefully asked, "Is it... Dyanne?"

"It's Fred. They said he committed suicide!" Oh my God, oh my God, oh my God! He had just gotten the call and tried between his emotional sobs to explain what he had been told. This afternoon—about 12:30. "Mom, he didn't mean it." *NO! NO! NO!!*

We left immediately for home, and I was partly on the floorboard of the car, bent over moaning and cradling my body, praying. Oh, God, sent your angels, send your angels, protect my baby, oh God, nooooo! Oh, Freddy, no! I heaved; I screamed over and over without making a sound; I couldn't breathe. My heart was breaking. It can't be! No, don't let this be true! No, no, it can't be!

September 27, 1994, my 28-year-old son Freddy died. It was not a suicide, as first assumed, and we still don't have all the answers surrounding his death. The Los Angeles sheriff's department came and did some kind of knee-jerk assessment, assuming a suicide from jumping off a one-story deck. Even an amateur could figure out that a young, physically active, 28-year-old man would have a very difficult time committing suicide by jumping one story. *I* could jump one story and perhaps break a leg or arm—maybe if I were trying, I *might* break my neck—but it would be almost impossible to actually commit suicide.

There were other rumors but none that we could confirm. And the question remained—what really happened?

The days following his death were extremely difficult, sometimes a nightmarish fog, sometimes so real that I couldn't breathe. Sometimes I had to will myself to breathe. The grief didn't diminish. I prayed, I wept, and I was inconsolable. I wanted to die, too, and I spiraled into despair.

Brothers Eric (left) and Fred

Even though I had other precious children, all grieving the tremendous loss of their brother, I felt that my life was over. How could I go on when my child was dead? The sadness was like a heavy blanket engulfing my entire body, choking off my breathing and weighing like a vise against my chest. Even now, years later, when I remember or talk about his death, I choke up and my throat constricts sometimes to the point that I can't speak. I prayed, or rather, cried in my spirit, in my heart, "God please help me through this! Please give me some comfort! Please help me, I can't bear this pain!"

I felt as if my body, my legs, were literally sinking into the ground. I had no strength, my thoughts were cloudy, and the question always returned: *Why?* The hope would linger at night that I would go to sleep and wake up and find it had merely been a nightmare. But there was no comfort—not from family, loved ones, books, friends; every word spoken, every expression of sympathy, every comment seemed empty. The only numbing comfort I could find was reading my Bible. I would read or stare as in a trance for hours at a time.

I have come to believe, after suffering all kinds of death and pain, that there is no pain that can compare to the death of a child.

THE SOUND OF WINGS

Three days after my son was buried, Dave felt that we needed to visit Dave's close friend Paul Troyer, who was in hospice care facing cancer and the final days of his life. Paul had been in a semi-catatonic state for awhile and had not responded to visitors or other stimulus. I was dreading the visit, afraid that I might break down, but Paul had been such a dear friend it was something we needed to do.

Dave sat on one side of the bed and I was on the other, Paul stared straight ahead—he didn't blink, change his facial expression, or look to the right or left. He didn't respond in any way as Dave tried to carry on a one-sided conversation with him. He seemed to be in a "death trance," staring at the light moving on the TV. Dave was just trying to make conversation, and finally, Dave asked Paul if he would like me to pray for him. My eyes widened as I gave Dave a glaring look and I almost choked. How could Dave do that to me, knowing the frame of mind I was in? I swallowed, took a deep breath and silently said, "God help me."

I didn't want to pray, but I couldn't say no to this request. I took Paul's hand held it in mine and began to pray. How do you pray for someone who is in the last moments of life? I didn't know, but I knew or felt that he would know if I was phony and said the flowery things that people tend to pray when they have to pray out loud. To pray for healing? How could I pray for that?

God, please give me the right words, I said in my heart, and began, "Father, you know our hearts. I pray that now in these final hours, you will send your comforting Spirit, that you will send your angels to bring comfort and peace to Paul, that you will take his hand and gently lead him and cover him with the warmth of your presence. Let him know that you are here and take away all fear, and embrace him in your arms."

As I was praying, I began to hear the fluttering sound of wings. The tears that I couldn't contain began to fall on Paul's hand as I continued, and I could see Paul turn toward me looking directly at me, but I don't think he was seeing me—there was a different expression on his face, and as I finished, he whispered softly, "Thank you."

Paul continued to stare at me, and as we left, his eyes followed me even out the door. We talked with Paul's wife, and I asked her if she had seen the way Paul responded and if she had heard the sound of wings as we were praying. She said she was very surprised to see how Paul had responded because he had not been at all responsive for almost a week, and his reaction did seem very strange.

I can't explain what happened or why. But to me, it felt as if Paul were surrounded by God's angels who came to bring comfort to him in his final hours—to embrace him. We think of angels with wings, and as strange as it might seem, I believe that God let me hear the sound of those wings, and by that sound, I knew that this prayer was being answered. Paul died peacefully the next day.

PART THREE

The Voice..."How can I stay silent when I hear
you call my name?" Lord, make it very clear.

CHAPTER VIII

I grew up in a family that had a quiet but strong faith—"Evidence of things not seen."

On the third weekend after my son's death, my husband decided to take me on a three day "escape" trip, driving our newly purchased motor home to a camp ground in the Colorado National Monument area, a beautiful and colorful canyon with dramatic views and wind-twisted pines and cedar trees on the outskirts of Grand Junction, Colorado.

I didn't want to go. I didn't want to go or do anything. I resented that we had a brand new motor home that we had ordered and had picked up the week before my son died.

But I went.

That weekend was the weekend that would begin the healing of my heart and eventually change the focus of my life.

I've been told that a person suffering from grief experiences many things that they can't always explain; some may be real and some perceived because of the tenderness of their spirit during this time. I know that I was suffering the pain of grief and not a psychological disorder. I can't give you spiritual reasons or scientific explanations.

I can only assure you that I believe these things were real and for a purpose, and I will share that with you.

The evening of the first day of our stay in Colorado National Monument Park, my husband and I went for a walk to the canyon overlook. While standing there in the beauty of the area, I was jolted to hear a voice—a soft voice, but clearly speaking the words, "Feed... my...children."

I thought at first that it must be my imagination, I asked my husband, "Did you hear anything? A voice, rustling of the leaves?"

"No," he said and asked, "Why?"

"Well, I know you're going to think I'm crazy, but I just heard a voice say 'Feed my children'."

He didn't say anything but looked at me like—well, like I was crazy. My native insecurity kicked in, and I thought, "Perhaps I am hallucinating or going slightly crazy," so I didn't say anything else.

The next afternoon as I was walking alone taking photos of some of the unusually shaped trees, I stopped to take a second look and photo of a larger tree standing alone in the center of the path. As I stood there looking, I heard the same voice and the same words: "Feed...my...children."

This time I felt I had to take the experience seriously. Either I was suffering from serious effects of extreme emotional distress, or that voice was real, and I needed to pay attention. This experience happened before being bipolar became so common. Actually I had not even heard of bipolar, so that possibility didn't even cross my mind.

I returned to our motor home and began researching everything I could find regarding God speaking to someone. I read in John 21 where Jesus asked Peter, "Do you love me?" Each time Peter affirmed his love, Jesus gave a different response: "Feed my lambs," "Take care of my sheep," and "Feed my flock."

I asked, "Is this what I'm looking for?" But the words I heard were so specific. "Feed...my...children." I had to keep looking.

When I read the story of Samuel and Eli (in I Samuel 3), I saw that God called Samuel's name, but Samuel thought it was the priest Eli calling him. The second time when Samuel went to Eli to respond, Eli gave Samuel instructions, "If the Lord calls again, answer, speak Lord, for your servant is listening."

That was my answer. If this were a voice from my own imagination, I would not hear it again—but if it were a call or the voice of God or His spirit? If this were the Lord trying to get my attention, then I knew it would happen a third time, and I knew how I would answer.

On the third afternoon, while resting and trying to read a book, I was again interrupted with the same quiet voice and the same words, "Feed...my...children."

This time I responded and said, "Lord, I hear your voice. I am your servant, and I am willing to do whatever you are calling me to do. But I don't know what you want me to do, and I don't want to imagine or make up something that I suppose you want. I am asking you to be very clear with your instructions so that I am sure I am doing what You want."

I had no idea what the words meant for me, but I soon discovered that my life would never be the same.

Weeks went by, and I continued in my life of mourning. I didn't forget the voice or the promise, but I was determined not to force the answers through my own ideas.

EVEN THE ANGELS WEEP

I had always felt confident in the promise of eternal life and God's hand in all things, but now I was facing a devastating reality. Why did my son die? Then what happened to him? Where *is* he? God, are You really real? Is this all there is? Will I see my son again? Those questions and the grief that accompanied them set me on a spiritual quest and journey that continues to this day. Even though the following pages may seem long this is only a very small piece of that journey and the story that has been weaving through my life.

One very cold winter night in November, with temperatures in the single digits, filled with grief and depression to the point of wanting to end my own life, I left my house about 9 P.M. and told my husband that I was going to the little gallery that we owned. I had no intention of going there. In despair and hopelessness, I was thinking to drive off and never return. But then I thought, "It is really cold. What if I do something that just makes me more miserable, or deformed, or crippled? Perhaps I should think this through." I drove into a Wendy's parking lot in the West Vail area to think it through.

There was only one car in the lot, and I noticed the snow had been plowed and was stacked high to six or seven feet around the parking area. I drove to the order window and ordered a small frosty so that I could park without people wondering what I was doing. I parked next to the single car that was there, the ice crystals forming on their windows, clear skies typical of this type of cold.

I turned off my car and heater then sat for 30 to 45 minutes with tears pouring down my face, crying in painful prayer. Most of the time I was not even able to do more than moan and hold myself as I rocked back and forth in the seat. "God, I have always believed that You are real, I have always had faith, but now I need a sign, assurance that You *are* real, that my son is with you, that he is okay, and that I will see him again."

As I lifted my head, I looked at the windshield. Drops of water began to splash and stream down the windshield, drops like rain pouring from the sky.

I looked at the car on my right side with the ice crystals still on the windows—no rain there. I turned on my windshield wipers and tried to rationalize what might be happening. I knew it wasn't snow melting off the roof of the car. It was 4° outside, and the car and heater had been off for almost 45 minutes.

Then, almost as suddenly as it started, it stopped, and a sense of peace engulfed me. Warmth spread through my body, and in my spirit I felt that God *had* given me a sign. I felt that He had answered my prayers. *"I hear your cry, and even the angels in heaven weep over the loss of a child."* It seemed as if tears from heaven were falling on my windshield. I don't expect others to believe, but whatever actually happened that night, for me it was an answer, and it was real.

CHAPTER IX

THE KEY

He who opens doors, no man can close.

Have you ever considered the significance of a key? We use it in symbolism a lot: the Key to the City; the key to happiness; the key to my heart; the key figure; on key/off key; key note speaker; a key stone; and so on. The other day I was looking at a magazine ad for Tiffany's, and it showcased three beautiful but very different keys...the catchy description said, "The Key...An intriguing invitation. A revealing discovery. A promise of adventure. A question answered ...A secret Key."

In history, the "holder of the keys" had a lot of power—he could lock out intruders, attackers, or other unwanted visitors to a city; he could literally shut people in and shut people out.

In the book of Revelations, we read,

These things saith He that is Holy, He that is True, He that hath the key of David, He that openeth, and no man shutteth: And shutteth,

and no man openeth. I know thy works: Behold, I have set before
you an open door, and no man can shut it.

One day in late November, I went to our gallery to work. It was
the first time I had returned to work since Freddy's death. Because it
was such a slow time of year in the Vail area, I was alone most of that
cold, snowy day. I had cried on my way to work and was hoping that
no one would come in.

However, it was not going to be a day without visitors. In the early
afternoon I looked out the front window and saw a young woman
striding up the walk. I thought to myself, "She has a purpose; she is
coming to buy something!"

As we greeted each other with the familiar, "How are you?" "Fine,
how are you?" etc., she looked at me and insisted, "How are you *really*?"

Surprised by the seriousness and intensity of her question, I responded honestly by telling her that my son had died unexpectedly
in September and some days were more difficult than others.

Continuing to hold my attention, she said, "I know, I felt the need
to stop here today and felt there was someone who needed prayer.
Do you mind if I pray for you?"

I have to admit that I was uncomfortable with the idea of someone praying for me, especially in public in a business environment. I
glanced out the window again to make sure no one else was in the
area before saying, "Please, go ahead."

She began to pray and her prayer was very different than any I
had heard before. She was praying about me and spoke of things that
God was speaking to me, of things that no one knew but God and me.

As she finished praying, we talked briefly, and then she put her
hands over my heart and began to pray again. "God has placed a key
in your heart," she said. "I don't know the significance of the key, but
He will reveal this to you in time." As she was speaking I was thinking
of the other events that had happened to me in the past two months
and wondered what she was talking about. But I didn't mention
those things to her. I was relieved when she finally stopped praying.

Then she knelt and began to pray again, over my feet. I come from "big stock," people with big bones, big hands, big feet. I had black cowboy boots on and felt that my feet must have looked ten feet long.

"Your feet will carry a message of *hope* and *peace*," she said. I responded with "Oh, Lord, please don't send me to Africa—I'm too old!" Then she said, "Nothing was said about Africa, only that your feet will carry a message of *hope* and *peace*. God's spirit will give you the answer when the time is right."

Several more weeks passed, and I went on with my life, preparing for the Christmas season in Vail. One late afternoon, the same young woman who had prayed for me came into our gallery. I saw her at a distance and greeted her. As I walked toward her I saw the key that she had around her neck. Without knowing why, I pointed at the key and said, "Is that my key?"

She looked surprised and held the key tightly, as if to protect it. Feeling foolish for making that comment, I started apologizing. "I was just kidding. I don't know why I said that." She looked at the key, then closed her eyes as if in prayer. She then looked at me and said, "Yes, this is your key." I was embarrassed because she took very seriously what I thought was a joke. I refused to take the key as she handed it to me. But she insisted and said, "It is your key; you must take it."

As I held the key in my hand she said, "Now let me tell you the story of this key."

She began, "One afternoon in Salt Lake City, I had planned to meet with friends at a coffee house. When I arrived, I noticed a "street" man waiting outside. He followed us in and stood at the table next to us. I felt compelled to invite him to join us for a cup of coffee. We talked for a few minutes and then he pulled out a map from his back pack. He drew a circle in the center of the map where my home town is. Then he proceeded to tell me all the areas that I had been in my walk with God, the places I had traveled. He then drew lines to the center circle, and showed me that the path I had traveled was the shape of a cross. I asked him how he knew where I had been and what I had been doing. He smiled and said, "God sees what we do." It was at that point I noticed the key he was wearing around his neck. I boldly grabbed it and said, 'Is that my key?'"

Continuing with her story, she said, "He looked at me, laughed, and took the key from around his neck to give it to me, saying, 'Yes, this is your key.' He went on to say, 'This is a very special key, and I am giving it to you. God will reveal the significance of the key to you, and you will know when it is time to give it away.' Nancy," she continued, "I knew this man was not an ordinary man but a messenger or angel from God."

As she concluded her story, I examined the key closely. I saw an angel face and wings, a nine ball crown and seven arches, a beautiful and intricate key—but there were no sudden revelations for me. I wore the key for the next few weeks, looking at it from time to time, searching for a special meaning and wondering if there was any truth to what I had been told.

Frustrated by my lack of inspiration or revelation regarding the significance of the key I asked my older brother who had been a minister "What does the number nine mean, in a spiritual sense?" He thought for a moment and then replied. "It does seem that in God's universe and plan numbers have different significance, the number nine seems to represent God's power. The number three representing the power of God in trinity, nine being a perfect number, three times three equals nine, three plus three plus three equals nine, nine times three equals twenty seven which added together still equals nine, etc." I was not particularly listening to all of the detail because he had lost me, and the first statement seemed the most important. "That's it!" I said, "God's power!" But what significance did it have for me, or for this key?

Little by little, it seemed that God was revealing answers to me like pieces of a puzzle. I contented myself with this and waited for more.

THE VISIT...THE ANOINTING?

For over a year I had suffered a great deal of intermittent pain, a burning that went all the way through my body radiating in the middle of my back. I had gone to various doctors trying to find an answer, and it was beginning to seem there wasn't an answer. Then a doctor was recommended to me who assured me that he would find the answer, and he did. My big pain was a little gall stone that needed to be removed. All right! Let's do it; get this over with! The surgery was scheduled.

The night before my surgery I was feeling anxious for some reason, and told Dave, "I just don't feel very good about going in for surgery tomorrow," but I prepared to do it.

A very strange thing happened about 3 A.M. during the early hours of the day I was to have surgery. Something woke me, and I sensed that someone was in our room—a presence of some kind. At first I had the thought, "Is that my grandmother?" (I don't know why I thought of my grandmother, who had passed away about ten years earlier.) I was trying to see or feel what it might be. I wasn't afraid, I just couldn't figure out what was happening. Then there was this overwhelming aroma that filled the room, a sweet spicy aroma. What is it? I wondered. I thought Dave must have cologne on, and I was sniffing his pillow and nuzzled up to his back to see if that was where the aroma was coming from, but it wasn't Dave. Finally, I drifted back into sleep but surrounded by the peaceful feeling of that aroma.

The next morning, we arrived at the hospital and did all the fun things that have to be done before surgery, clothes off, backwards gown on, paper shoes on the feet, and an ugly paper hat on my head. Then it was time to start the IV.

The nurse kept trying to put the needle in my arm. It didn't work. She finally moved to the wrist to start the IV. The needle bent, and she freaked out. The anesthesiologist came in and did a little interview, and then he said, "We're not going to do surgery on you today."

Why? He didn't give me any answer but "We're not going to do surgery on you today." I grabbed my things and went home, relieved.

Later that same day, I was visiting with a friend in my kitchen when I heard a knock on my door. I was surprised to see Anita, the mother of a friend of my youngest son, standing at the door crying. "What's happened?" I asked and embraced her.

She sobbed as she explained that she had talked her next door neighbor, her very best friend, into getting a hysterectomy after so many years of discomfort. "This morning in surgery something happened. An artery was hit and my friend bled to death, died on the operating table." The same operating table that I was scheduled to be on that morning. It was the first death of this kind at the Vail hospital and quite a sobering thought for me because I had been scheduled to go into surgery just before that tragedy happened.

Seeing the terrible distress that she was in, I asked Anita if we could pray for her. My friend brought out a bottle of anointing oil and asked if she could anoint her as she prayed. As she put the oil on Anita's forehead I suddenly recognized the aroma. It was the aroma that had permeated my bedroom in the night.

Is it ridiculous to wonder whether—if I had been the one to go into surgery that morning, as was scheduled—*I* might have been the one who died on the operating table? Or is it too strange to think that the visit in the night and the aroma that permeated the room was some kind of protective presence? I can't answer that question. I only know that I felt that somehow I had been spared.

WARNING FOR MY DAUGHTER

At Christmas in 1992, an unusual incident happened that (now) seems to tie into some future events, when my daughter, who had been living in Switzerland while working and studying German, had returned home for a visit.

During her stay in Switzerland, she had become involved in a very controlling relationship, which she finally reluctantly admitted to us. She acknowledged that her life had been threatened if she didn't return. "I'll hunt you down; there are places where I can hide you and no one will ever find you!" She was afraid not to return and afraid to return.

One day during that holiday season I was working alone at the gallery and a young man, close to seven feet tall with a full head of long, curly, blond hair, bright blue eyes, and a contrasting light tan complexion came in. I have to admit that I was slightly taken back by his size and striking good looks. I talked to him for a few minutes and asked him where he was from. "South Africa," he said.

At that moment, the gallery phone rang, so I went to answer it. It was my daughter's boyfriend calling from Europe to see where she was and to see how he could reach her. I don't remember what excuse I gave him, but I didn't acknowledge that I was her mother or that I knew where she was or how to reach her.

When I returned I apologized to the young man, explaining that it was my daughter's boyfriend, Goran, wanting to find her. I mentioned that I was concerned for her safety and her life, because he had threatened her if she didn't return. I repeated what my daughter told me Goran had said: that he would find her and take her where no one could ever find her again. Without hesitation the young man asked, "He is Croatian, isn't he?" I was surprised, because that was exactly what he was.

His father was Serbian and his mother a Croatian from Bosnia, but he was living in Switzerland. "And," this young man continued, "he will not hesitate to do what he threatens. I know these people. They mean what they say, and you must get your daughter away from him as quickly as possible." I was speechless for a few minutes as I tried to regain my composure from the statements he had made. How did he know where her boyfriend was from, only from a name? I hadn't mentioned where he was from. How did he know these things, and why would he say them to me, a stranger?

Dave and I talked with our daughter and made a quick decision to buy tickets and fly back with her before she was expected to arrive. We would fly into Zurich and drive so that we could slip into the city where she had her apartment and her personal things.

We went fast, closed her bank account, went to her apartment, and quickly packed her clothes. As we were packing her things the landlady came in and started complaining and yelling at her about leaving, but we kept our course, took her things, and got her away. We headed to Belgium and out of Frankfort back to the U.S.

It was a wild trip, but I believe that if it hadn't been for that beautiful young man from South Africa—or wherever he might have really been from—we would not have recognized the immediate danger and had the courage to rescue our daughter from this extreme situation.

I have come to believe more firmly throughout these years that we sometimes do entertain angels unaware.

THE VISION

Call unto Me and I will answer you, and show you Great and Mighty things, which you know not.

Jeremiah 33:3

Several weeks later, I was once again in the gallery with two employees—a Native American artist from the Taos Pueblo, a Jewish woman, and myself, a Christian. We were three very different people with very different spiritual beliefs, yet we were discussing spirituality and some unusual things that had happened in the past months.

As part of that conversation I was talking about the key, the number nine, and how three plus three plus three (3 + 3 + 3) could represent God's Power.

Without thinking I said, "It's like Jeremiah 33:3! That's it! That's the significance of the number nine—three plus three plus three!" and I quoted the verse from somewhere in my memory: "Call unto Me and I will answer you, and show you Great and Mighty things, which you know not."

But what is the significance of that for me?

The following months were full of unusual events that continued to add pieces to the puzzle that seemed to be growing larger and larger. However, it wasn't until the following March—1995—that the puzzle began to form into a real picture and started to take clear shape.

CHAPTER X

EXPERIENCE IN FRESNILLO

February 2, 1995, my husband and I began the long drive from Colorado to Manzanillo in southern Mexico where we have our home. We normally left Colorado right after the Christmas holiday and New Year, but this year was different. It had been difficult to make plans and have the energy to put everything in order so that we could leave for the winter. I was struggling emotionally, barely functional, and had no desire to travel anywhere.

The trip is about 1,800 miles, and we usually planned three to four days. We had our favorite places to stop and looked forward to seeing the changes of scenery and climate as we traveled through the dry desert mountains, passing the Tropic of Cancer and then into the more tropical mountainous terrain.

We took different routes throughout the years just for variety or to see new country, but the fastest and most familiar route was through El Paso, Texas, and Juarez, Mexico. We would travel down the northern state of Chihuahua, normally stopping in either the city of

Chihuahua or Camargo for the first night in Mexico, then on to Fresnillo or Zacatecas.

On this trip we had my mother and her fourth husband Paul traveling with us. Paul was a wonderful man, and I wonder why it had
taken her so long to find him. He was from Switzerland, had traveled
all over the world, spoke six or seven languages fluently, and took
her on adventures that she never could have dreamed of as a stay-at-
home housewife back in Houston, Texas. At fifty, she learned German
and studied Spanish. They toured all of Europe and entertained
friends with their different styles of cooking, she was an excellent
south Texas style cook, and he was a trained Swiss chef. Finally, she
had found someone who loved her and appreciated what a special
person he had.

Mother and Paul loved to travel to Mexico with us. They brought
their little dog, Pete, and we brought our bigger little dog, Ninjie. We
would travel either in the same vehicle or caravan with two cars. On
this trip, we were traveling together and decided it was too late to
drive the extra two hours in the dark, so we pulled into a large hotel
complex on the outskirts of Fresnillo called La Fortuna, on the Car-
retera Panamericana in the state of Zacatecas.

We had stayed at this motel each time we stopped in Fresnillo. It
had an area with buildings set like little duplexes or cabanas and that
made it easier for us to slip in with the dogs.

We checked in, had a late dinner at the restaurant, and went to
bed, each of us on our side of the duplex.

I have engraved in my memory the setting of that room. Dave
was asleep and snoring on my right side. There was a dresser with a
lamp across the room. The bathroom opened into the bedroom, and
the bedroom wall facing the drive was solid without windows. This
memory is so important to me because it was in this room on that night
about 3 A.M. that a soft light woke me, becoming brighter and brighter
as I lay there watching, listening to Dave's snores. Then suddenly my
lost son, Freddy, was standing at the foot of the bed.

It was as if my spirit left my body and went directly to him. "Oh Freddy, I didn't get to say goodbye," I cried, and as we fell into a warm embrace, he said, "I know, Mom." I can't explain how this all happened. The communication was not vocal but seemed to be between our spirits. "Freddy, I love you so much," I wept, and he just gently replied, "I love you too, Mom." Then—all this was within what must have been less than a moment—he said, "I have to go now." He was gone, and I was lying in the bed with my husband beside me still snoring.

I am very reluctant to relay this experience because there have been some fellow Christians who have condemned this type of event as being "demonic." Truthfully, it takes a lot of courage for me to relate this today, even though it was the one event that helped to heal the pain of not being able to say goodbye to my son. The feeling I had was one of warmth and peace, not fear or distress.

Regardless of whatever happened in the early hours of that morning in Fresnillo, whatever I believe happened, or what others might believe happened, for me it was a gift—a blessing that could only come from God.

Several years later I spent time with a psychologist who specialized in grief counseling, and I was surprised to hear him say, "I believe that was a real experience, a gift." He explained to me, "This is not an unusual experience for people who have lost a loved one, especially a loved one who was emotionally close to them." I have been amazed to hear from others throughout the years who have had similar experiences.

The next morning we continued our trip to Manzanillo. Dave was, quite naturally, uncomfortable as I told him about the experience of the early morning, and although he didn't discuss this, we have never returned to that motel or stayed in Fresnillo again. I drove down seven years later with several other women and asked if we could stop at La Fortuna in Fresnillo for the night so that I could confirm in my mind that my memory of that room was correct. One reason that this return stop was important to me was that I thought perhaps the light shining into the room might have been headlights from a car. But the room was as I remembered—without windows on the street side. It would have been impossible for any kind of light to shine into the room from the outside.

Manzanillo is a beautiful place. I've been told that it is the same latitude as Hawaii, and that the temperature doesn't change more than 3° up or down during most of the year. It is the humidity that changes, and in the rainy season, you feel like you are in a 100° sauna. Each evening or afternoon, the torrential rains come, bringing a cool relief, but sometimes with such force the streets fill with water up to the running boards of the cars before it finally runs off.

Manzanillo truly is a semi-tropical paradise with sandy beaches, mountainous backdrop, palm trees, and flowers. It is also one of the largest ports on the Pacific Ocean.

I didn't realize, nor had I thought about the fact, that with a large port also comes a higher incidence of prostitution, drugs, alcohol abuse, and child trafficking. With these problems, the number of abused, deprived, and abandoned children grows tremendously.

The beautiful side of Manzanillo

I was soon going to be shown a darker world and witness first-hand the tragedy and courage of thousands of children, suffering in silence on the streets, in the houses, in the community dumps, and in places only fit for animals.

SHARING THE VISION WITH FELIPE: "IT IS FROM GOD"

One Tuesday afternoon in March, my husband asked me to lie down and rest with him for awhile. I never take naps, but I reluc-tantly laid down. Just as I started to drift off I felt as if someone, or something, was pulling me up, and I once again heard a voice in my soul: "You have to build an orphanage—*here!*" I sat up, startled. As the thoughts flooded my mind, I felt compelled to get off the bed, grab a pen and tablet, and move outside onto the upper terrazzo. I begin writing as quickly as I could, as if God was speaking directly and clearly to me.

"I have heard the cries of the children, and I will answer them. I (the Lord God) will provide. I will touch the hearts of those who will come. It will be through My power and My spirit that this will happen; each item, each person will be provided when the time is right."

When I finished writing, I was exhausted. I thought, "Where did this come from?" But in my heart, in my spirit, I had no doubt. These were not my ideas, these were not my plans, my designs, my desires. I had no doubt this was from God.

I sat on the terrazzo while Dave was still sleeping, contemplating what I had just experienced. It was during this time that a young friend, Felipe, came into the yard area that the terrazzo overlooks. Felipe, a friend of our son, had been part of our "Mexico family" for a number of years. As I saw him coming up the walk, I waved to him, softly called, and put my finger to my lips for him to be quiet. "Felipe, come up here."

He slipped into the door and tiptoed past Dave and then onto the terrazzo. Eager to share the things that had happened, concluding with this latest experience, I began telling him all the events that had filled my life since Fred's death and the message I had just heard.

While I talked, Felipe was staring at me. I thought at first that he didn't understand. He had such a strange look on his face, and I asked, "Felipe, did you understand what I said?"

"Yes." Then he slowly and emphatically replied, "It is from God."

I answered, "Yes, I believe it is."

Then he said, "No, I mean—it is an answer from God. Last night, twenty-three members of my family and church prayed until almost three in the morning with our pastor—that God would help us find a way to help the children of Manzanillo. And today He has answered our prayers!"

I didn't say anything more to anyone other than my husband and wondered what was next.

A few days later I was jolted again from my afternoon rest, "Make the Key!" Then I began to understand. The key I had been given could be made in silver by my friend Juan Sotelo and silversmith Jesús in Taxco, Mexico. The key was somehow part of all of this, and perhaps silver copies of the key could be sold with proceeds going toward the orphanage.

Because I was told that there were only two keys exactly like this key, I made the decision to replace the cherub's face with a tear drop amethyst. For me the tear drop represented that freezing cold night when the "tear" drops fell on my windshield. I don't know if there are more keys exactly like this one—it really doesn't matter. For me the key is symbolic of God's calling and His answer to prayer.

The vision was firmly planted in my mind and on my heart. With faith and strength that can only come from facing a lack of faith and the weakness that comes from pain, I determined to begin moving forward, trusting that God would do as He had promised.

But I didn't know how to begin.

I was confident that this was the Lord's hand, and I was not going to ignore His call a second time. But the months slipped by.

For the first time I saw the reality of the streets filled with children. They were ragged children, dirty and without care. Many of these children had come from other parts of Mexico trying to find opportunity, hope, and when you looked closely, you could see the pain in their eyes and the blank expressions. Many of them were sniffing glue between washing car windows. Some would hold diesel in their mouths, lighting it at the same time as they spewed it out. They would do anything for a few pesos just to survive.

I have to say that I began to look at these children differently now than I had in the past. I used to say or think, just like most other people, "Look at that poor little thing" or "Isn't that a cute little boy washing my windshield." All of a sudden I began to look beyond the faceless groups of children, and I saw each child in a different way.

One morning a Mexican attorney, Raphael de La Colina R., a casual friend who lived a few blocks away from where we lived, called and asked if we were going into town that day and asked if he could catch a ride with us. I was heading to the store, so I picked him up, and during the drive I began to tell him about the death of my son, the voice, and the vision to build an orphanage.

I admitted my frustration because I didn't know where or how to begin but knew that I had to do this. After a few minutes of thoughtfulness, he replied to me, "Nancy, the first thing you have to do is take care of the legal papers and requirements." Then he continued, "Last November, our youngest son was killed in a motorcycle accident in Mexico City, and I would be honored to do all the legal work you will need for this project in memory of my son Gabriel."

Signing the paperwork to open Casa Hogar:
from left, Nancy, Monica Welter from Mexico City,
and Mexican attorney Rafael de la Colina.

The first matter that had to be taken care of was writing a constitution and building a board of directors.

People sometimes look and say, "Oh, I envy you. I would like to do what you are doing." But they really have no idea. There have been times when I faced fear and frustration so intense that I would lie in bed and shake or pace the floor in the middle of the night.

I would think to myself, "If I had known what I know now—what I would have to face and deal with—personally, financially, spiritually, legally, and physically—I would have wanted to suggest that perhaps the wrong person was called for this job. Then I would find myself holding tight to the firm conviction that God is faithful, and if He called me into this work, He would see me through it.

The stress of building a board of directors and founders for a non-profit organization in a foreign country was overwhelming. Suddenly, I had no fewer than thirty people wanting to be board members, wanting their name on the foundation. I didn't know what to do. I really didn't know any of the people well enough to know who should be on the board or who might cause serious problems later.

The night before I had to make some definitive decisions regarding the board configuration, I went to bed about 10:00 P.M. but tossed and turned and couldn't sleep. I got up, grabbed my Bible, and quietly went into the upper living area of our home in Manzanillo. I prayed, "Lord, please give me an answer to this dilemma. I don't know what to do or how to make this decision. Please send your Holy Spirit to guide me to a scripture or message that will give me some answers."

I know people who do this kind of thing all the time. They have a situation, or question and they say, "Okay, I'm going to flip open my Bible and take the answer I find in the first message I read." I don't do that. Or at least, *normally* I don't do that. However, this night I was at my wit's end, so in desperation I decided to take this leap of faith that God would help me in some way with an answer through His Word.

I closed my eyes and prayed again. As I opened my Bible and came face to face with the story of the Israelite Gideon, the theme of the message hit home. Gideon had been called to rescue his people against the oppression of great armies of the Midianites and Amalekites, armies so numerous they could not be counted. Gideon was able to raise a large army, but the Lord told him he had too many. He cut the army down until he had a group that numbered only three hundred. Gideon didn't need a large army, he only needed a few good men. My answer came in that message, "You don't need a large group of people, just a few good men that believe and are willing to serve." (Judges 6–8)

"GOD HAS ENTRUSTED US WITH GREAT SORROW"

One year after my son died, we received a call from my younger sister, 35 years old, crying as she told us that she had cancer and it had spread to other parts of her body. She was taken to intensive care in Kansas City where she lived. It was October, and we were traveling in Sweden with my mother and Paul when we received the call. We drove immediately from Sweden into Germany, and Mother and I flew back from Frankfurt, landed at DIA (Denver International Airport), picked up the van that my daughter had dropped off for us, and took off in a blizzard, driving I-70 east straight through to Kansas City to be with her.

"There is little hope; her cancer has metastasized." The doctors decided to do a series of chemo, but the insurance counselor wouldn't recommend paying for any additional treatment. We desperately tried to find a way to save her life. When the doctors refused to try any other treatment in Kansas City, we made the decision to pick her up in our motor home, drive her to Denver, and bring her into the emergency room at the University of Denver Hospital. They were working on experimental treatment for certain types of cancer, and we hoped that she might be a candidate for this new treatment.

The day the doctor came in to tell her that he didn't feel she was a candidate for this new treatment, my sister removed her oxygen mask and within a short time her young life was ended. Her death was terribly painful, and within two months of discovering her cancer, she was dead.

At first my mother had a difficult time accepting that God didn't heal her daughter. She believed that a miracle would happen, even until the very end. I wondered at the time if this would push my mother into bitterness and anger toward God. It seems that people can easily lose their faith or become bitter. They believe that God will answer their prayers by healing their child, husband, or loved one, and then when they don't see the answer that they prayed for, they are devastated and disillusioned. That is a hard one to try to answer. How do we keep our faith in situations like that?

We have choices in life—not always over circumstances but instead over how we react to those circumstances. My mother gathered her strength together,and, in a renewed show of determination and faith several months later, wrote these words to her friends and family:

> God has entrusted us with great sorrow in the past five years. First we lost a precious son and grandson, Jacob Thomas, in a skiing accident. Then, in September, 1994, we lost another precious son and grandson, Freddy. On January 2, 1996, we lost a precious daughter, Vicki D'Cille, a mother, sister, and wife. Through this sorrow, God has provided a way to keep their memories alive and their deaths not in vain....God has opened wonderful doors of opportunity here in the Manzanillo, Mexico area. Since our arrival on January 22, 1996, we have had a busy time. We are grateful for the love of God and for the amazing work that has been accomplished here....

Instead of allowing herself to go into bitterness and depression, as so many times we tend to do when suffering with such sadness and grief, my beautiful mother put her heart and energy into helping with the beginning and development of Casa Hogar Los Angelitos, rescuing children and feeding the hungry—a testimony to her faith and strength.

> We are made wise not by the recollection of our past, but by the responsibility for our future.
>
> George Bernard Shaw

PART FOUR

Feed the hungry, and help those in trouble.
Isaiah 58:9 (NLT)

CHAPTER XI

In James 2:15–17, it says, "If a brother or sister is naked and destitute of daily food, and one of you say to them, 'Go in peace, be warm and filled'; and you don't give them those things which are needed...What good is that?"

It was already November of 1995, and every direction we took ended with a dead end. We couldn't get a permit to open our doors; we had lost the property that had been promised to us, and I didn't know what to do next.

I had met with Saúl Gonzales, pastor of Felipe's church, and he made a statement to me that made me stop. "What did the Lord say to you, Nancy? "Feed My Children," right? So, maybe it's time to start feeding the children." With the encouragement of young Felipe and Pastor Saúl, I decided, "Okay, it's time to do something—anything."

Felipe, Pastor Saúl, and I drove through a poor area of Salagua, looking for a place to begin feeding street children. While we were driving, I saw a small two-story building on the corner of one of the streets. It looked abandoned, grass grown up around it, in need of repair, and paint. I turned to Felipe and said, "That is the kind of building that would be ideal to begin this project; perhaps, if we went to the owner, agreed to fix it up, and pay the utilities, we could begin feeding children here."

Felipe looked at the building and then looked back at me, and said, "That building belongs to my father."

Felipe's father, Indalecio, agreed to lend us that building for only the cost of us painting and repairing it and paying the utilities.

> God doesn't ask us to do great things. He asks us to do small things with great love.
>
> Mother Teresa

In November 1995, we began a food kitchen in the community of Salagua, providing daily nourishment for more than 125 extremely poor children while continuing to work with legal documents and permits necessary to open the doors of an orphanage. This was accomplished through the efforts of volunteers from the local church, who came every day to prepare and serve the meals, and Felipe, who drove to the different businesses throughout the community asking for small donations of food in order to meet those needs. We used that building for almost five years. During those years, we fed hundreds of children.

Our first home—the comedor

We opened a second food kitchen—a *comedor*—the following year in Santiago and operated this food kitchen for four years. We faced unbelievable resistance and road blocks. There were ridiculous rumors and legal harassment. Through all of this, even in the initial stage, we were able to bring awareness to the community for the need to help the "street" children, the extremely poor, the abandoned, and the abused.

Above: The comedor in Salagua after painting and repair

Below: A group of volunteers from Houston

ARTURO AND BENJAMIN

It was almost midnight. We were driving back from the restaurant after a night of food and laughter when I noticed two raggedy, skinny little boys climbing into a large trash container each with a large bag that looked like it was half full of something.

Eating at the Comedor in 1995—Arturo
with other children and volunteer cooks

I thought I recognized the boys climbing in and out of that filthy dumpster, and then I realized who they were. It was the little brothers, Arturo and Benjamin, who had been coming to the comedor each day.

The next day at the comedor, I watched Arturo and Benjamin run across the street in their bare feet, torn shirts flapping open and faces still grimy from the dirt and filth that they lived in, yet their smiles were bright with anticipation. They were running to eat. Arturo must have been about nine years old and Benjamin seven, though they were so little and skinny that they looked much younger.

Two days before, I had gone to the store and purchased shoes for both boys after I asked why they weren't in school like the other children. Arturo said, "We can't go to school because we don't have shoes." But now, I saw that they were still barefoot and not in school.

"Arturo y Benjamin, que pasa? Donde está los zapatos?" Without missing a bite of food, Arturo, the older brother, explained, "My stepmother took them to Tecoman and sold them." It was as normal an answer as if it might be a daily event. "But those were for you and Benjamin," I protested. Arturo shrugged his thin shoulders and kept eating as fast as he could.

That afternoon, after all the children had finished eating, I took the boys to their "home." I had to weave around through the back streets, park at the end of the road, and walk along the drainage ditch to find the stick lean-to that was home to Arturo, Benjamin, and their family. There were five more younger siblings at that time, a drunken father, and a pregnant step-mother living in this small wretched hovel. It was about 10 x 12 feet and looked more like a stick fence. The shelter was braced against a wall that belonged to someone else's house. It had plastic and cardboard covering parts of it.

What water they had was taken out of the dirty drainage ditch. They must have used the side area for their bathroom, and there was a little area in front of the door with a few sticks stacked for cooking over a little dugout area.

Little by little I learned more about the life that Arturo and Benjamin had to live. The night that we saw them crawling into the commercial trash bin was typical of every night for them. At dark their father would send them out, each with a sack, to go rummaging through garbage bins throughout the community, behind stores and along the streets, looking for aluminum cans and edible food. Some nights they would return at midnight or later, and if their sacks weren't full enough, they would be beaten and sent back out on the streets. Children like Arturo and Benjamin are called *pordioseros*—

beggers, the worst kind: those who rummage through the garbage just to survive.

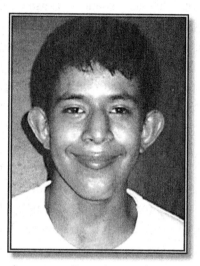

Arturo's sweet smile at the casa hogar in 2000

Arturo's ears were quite extended, and I saw he had a number of scars on his face. The things that these little boys had seen and had to live with, the abuse and neglect. They lived on the street, but the street, like the family they knew, was dangerous and mistreated them brutally. After being slammed in the head with a hot iron by his stepmother, Arturo began to have epileptic seizures, falling and cutting himself, breaking and bruising his nose more and more frequently.

His epilepsy was getting worse.

Each time I left Mexico and went back to the states trying to generate support and funding—trying to tell the story about the children —I would always keep Arturo and Benjamin's sweet grins and little faces with their big ears in my mind. Those little faces gave me the energy and inspiration to keep working towards the goal of opening the doors to the casa hogar.

CHAPTER XII

O nce people heard about the "Miracle in Manzanillo" and the vision, news reporters began to write editorials. The first one touched very poignantly on the horrible circumstances of the children living on the street. This editorial made a powerful statement, pointing out that the streets are full of children living like animals, and society turns it head, looking the other way.

> We call them the "street children" as if the streets gave birth to these children, but the streets didn't give birth to these children. They are the product of society, and it is society that needs to address this problem. (*El Correo*)

THE WONDER OF GOD'S POWER

It was during the early years that it seemed God's Spirit began "moving" in other areas of Manzanillo. Two religious groups that had been waiting as long as 20 years to "do something" realized that "now is the time." The city of Manzanillo began looking for ways to help street children, providing a place for street or transient children to sleep for up to 48 hours. People were finally becoming aware of the problems that many children in this area had to face every day.

Felipe and his sisters were an integral part of the comedors, looking for donations of food, cooking, and helping with the children.

During those early years it seems that there were so many "miracles" or unusual "coincidences."

ANGELICA

Little Angelica was eighteen months old and the youngest of a family of five little ones, the oldest being about seven years old. Her mother was a widow living in desperate circumstances with little food for her children. They all came to the comedor every day for their only meal of the day. The oldest was barely three feet tall, carrying little Angelica and dragging the three year old to wait their turn to eat that day's meal.

We noticed that it had been days since little Angelica came with the other children. It was as we opened the doors one morning, more than a week later, that Angelica's mother was outside waiting, holding little Angelica lethargically in her arms. Crying, she tried to explain that Angelica was very sick. The top of her head was extended with what was obviously a large growth in her skull. She couldn't stand or walk, had not been able to eat, and didn't even have the energy to cry from the pain.

We immediately called Doctora Maria Magaña, who had helped us in the past, to exam Angelica. "It appears to be a tumor or cist on her brain; she must be taken to Colima City to the social security hospital as soon as possible and be seen by a specialist." The doctor was explaining to Angelica's distraught mother, who desperately replied, "How can I do that? How can I even get there?"

Doctora Maria made the arrangements with the hospital, and we made arrangements for her transportation there and back. The exam was set for the following Monday. Wednesday night we met with Pastor Saúl to pray for Angelica, and during that prayer for some reason,

I spoke aloud the words "Help is on the way." I have no idea why or how that happened, it just popped out of my mouth.

Monday morning Angelica, in her mother's arms, left for Colima. After all the MRIs and exams, the diagnostic consensus was made: This was a cyst that had to be surgically removed as quickly as possible. Angelica was sent back home to prepare for surgery the following Monday.

Once again, we met to pray for little Angelica, and once again the words came: "Help is on the way." Angelica and her mother left early Monday morning to be ready for her surgery and arrived on time. Preparations were made, and another MRI was ordered before the surgery. The doctors checked and double checked and couldn't believe what they saw, or rather what they didn't see. There was no sign of a cyst, tumor, or any other problem in Angelica's brain.

The doctor actually wrote on Angelica's report, "It must be a miracle."

SELENÉ

Selené was about 11 years old at the time she was coming to the comedor to eat. She was a very thin girl who seemed to suffer from the same malnutrition that so many of the children suffered from. Her family was Mixteca Indians from the southern state of Guerrero, living in extreme poverty on the mosquito-infested river bed that runs through the community of Salagua. They walked the beach trying to eke out a small living selling their goods to tourists.

Because our program was very personalized, we worked with each child, knew their names, and kept a record of who came and when. We also were aware when children didn't come. These children were from extremely poor families or they were living on the street, and once they began coming they generally didn't miss those meals. Selené had missed several days and her brothers told Christie Pelayo, Felipe's sister, that Selené was very sick and had been taken to the civil hospital. Christie went directly to the hospital to find out what was wrong.

The doctors told her, "Selené has dengue hemorrhagic fever, and if she doesn't get help from another hospital—a private hospital that has better equipment than we have available—she may not live for more than several hours." Christie immediately called the house where Felipe and I were preparing to leave to look for donations of food out in the community. Christie pressed us. "We have to do something; we have to get her to Echauri Hospital where she can get the medication and care she needs to survive the internal bleeding; her vitals are already so low that she is not expected to live."

Felipe and I didn't have any time to find an ambulance, so we prayed for God's intervention and help and quickly left in our conversion van so we could transport Selené to the hospital. We called and told them we were going to be bringing in a patient who was in critical condition, and we roared out the door as fast as we could toward the civil hospital, arriving within fifteen to twenty minutes.

The civil hospital was at that time the place where people without money or social security went. Every area was as basic and bare as possible. So while the doctors were as competent as at other hospitals, they had little or no equipment.

Also, we knew Selené's type of dengue was extremely dangerous. It's caused by an infected mosquito bite, and if not treated immediately, the body begins to hemorrhage—that is, bleed uncontrollably—from all of the orifices: the ears, nose, eyes. There is also internal bleeding, and the person eventually succumbs. Once the disease has progressed to the point of hemorrhaging, the patient is in critical condition with perhaps 24–48 hours to live if there isn't immediate intervention with the appropriate treatment.

Christie met us at the door with the doctor. Expecting the worst, I was surprised and thrilled to hear them say, "We don't know what happened, but Selené suddenly had a reversal—the bleeding stopped and her vitals have improved tremendously. She has passed the crisis; she will live."

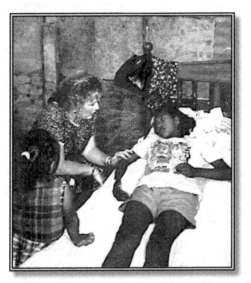

Selené at her home after leaving the civil hospital

We can choose to believe whatever we want to believe regarding the sudden and unexpected healing of both Angelica with her cyst and Selené with hemorrhagic dengue. I have no doubt in my mind that God held out His healing hand in both situations, intervening on behalf of the child.

Beware that you don't despise a single one of these little ones. For I tell you that in heaven their angels are always in the presence of my heavenly Father...

—Matthew 18:10

God provides the food...every day, even when we don't know from where or how it will come.

PUERTO VALLARTA

In fall 1996, I was asked to bring the vision and message "Feed My Children" to Pastor Saúl's church in Puerto Vallarta. We made the four-to-five-hour winding drive up the coast from Manzanillo to Puerto Vallarta, barely making it in time for the evening service.

That evening we were both surprised. Saúl was surprised because he assumed I would only speak for five to ten minutes, although he told me to take as much time as I needed. Obviously, he was not accustomed to having a woman speak before his congregation! And I was surprised because of the response by the women in the church when Saúl made the call, "Who will commit to this project? Who will help to feed the children?"

More than forty women came forward prepared to carry this vision, and it was that night the food program for children in Puerto Vallarta began. It is renamed "Children of the Dump" and had fed thousands of children; and there is also the "School of Champions," which provides basic education for these children and promotes the concept that every child is important to God.

LOURDES

It was January, and we were back in Vail getting ready to leave again, this time with a twelve-foot trailer in back of our van, loaded down with clothing, blankets, and food. Felipe had come up to visit and help present the project to various churches in Vail, Denver, and Loveland and then drive back with us.

We had collected and sorted the piles and piles of items—clothes, sweaters, blankets—that had been contributed by local charities for us to take down. Working until one in the morning, exhausted, we were asking ourselves, "Why are we taking all these sweaters and blankets down to tropical Manzanillo?!" Not wanting to reject any gift, we continued packing. We left about 6:00 A.M. on the icy, snow-packed roads to start our drive south through Leadville and Salida in order to make the first night in Alamosa.

We had made plans to visit Felipe's sister, Lourdes, who lived in Juarez, on the Mexico side of the border from El Paso. The roads had been snowy through Colorado but cleared up into New Mexico. Then we hit black ice as we were going into El Paso. I had never seen it so cold and icy in that part of Texas. Our trailer was sliding sideways as we edged our way down the incline of the road and across the bridge that takes us into Mexico.

Finally, Dave was able to get control of the slide, and we went across the bridge onto the Mexican side of the border. We prepared to check in at immigration and get our paperwork for the car and visas for us. As we pulled into the stall for inspection and the Mexican officer asked us what we had in the trailer, Felipe, now being a new Christian, felt he had to tell all. I had advised him to keep conversation to a minimum and not offer any information unless we had to— but not Felipe. "We are bringing all these clothes and blankets to the poor people in Manzanillo."

Well, suddenly it didn't matter whether we had papers showing that one nonprofit had contributed the items to our nonprofit.

"Sorry, it's illegal for you to bring those items across the border."

"What?" But, why? There was just no backing off. We went inside and sat for hours trying to convince the head man why we should be able to do this. We called our friends in Mexico City for them to help us. Nothing doing—no way were they going to allow us to take those items across on behalf of the "poor children in Manzanillo".

Finally, three hours later, I said, "Okay, we will go back to El Paso and donate everything to a church there." So we left with a plan. I am a little sorry to say that our plan was different than what we had told them, but close. We drove back across the border to El Paso and then the eight to ten miles to the cutoff that would take us through another border crossing twenty to thirty miles south and west of Juarez in the state of New Mexico.

This time I cautioned Felipe, "I know you feel compelled to just say all the truth, but please, this time don't say anything." We pulled into the border area and when the officer looked at the trailer, he asked the same questions. I answered perhaps not *quite* the truth—but mostly the truth.

"What do you have in there?"

"Just our things."

"Well, it seems like a lot."

"Yes, that's true."

"Adonde va?"

"Manzanillo."

"Well, I don't know," he said.

I could tell that he didn't have the confidence to make a firm decision either way, so I started shutting the door to the trailer and said, "Dios bendiga y gracias." He still had this funny look on his face and didn't say any more. I said to everyone, "Let's go; he's going to let us through." We all got in, and he never said another word as we began to drive forward. I wouldn't dare do that now, thinking there could be Federal Police waiting for us at the 50-kilometer checkpoint. I don't know how we did it, but there must have been a purpose.

The road we had to take to the 50-kilometer mark out of Juarez had very little traffic, and as we were driving, we began to see little shacks and lean-to's along the road. Shacks made from sticks and poles with cardboard coverings for roofs, where there even *was* a semblance of a roof. There were miles of these little shacks, stick shelters, not even fit for animals. The temperature was still freezing, and there was an icy snow still on the ground from the night before. These people were freezing to death, literally.

How could they survive in this temperature, huddled in those little one-room stick houses that didn't even have the protection of caulking between the sticks or glass on the windows? They were un-accustomed to this extreme and bizarre weather, but for us it was the conditions that they were living in that was unbelievable. We were shocked and simultaneously thought of finding a church or commu-nity center where we could leave the blankets and sweaters that we had stacked in the van to distribute to these freezing people.

We couldn't seem to find a church or any place that looked like a public building; in fact, we couldn't see anyone. It was strangely empty. We kept driving slowly, looking for a way to help, to find someone that would be available. We were trying desperately to de-termine what we would be able to do for these people.

It was several miles before we got to the main road out of Juarez when Felipe, looking at the housing off to the north said, "I think that is the area where my sister Lourdes lives."

"Are you sure?" I asked.

"Yes, I'm pretty sure. I've been there once before."

"Do you think you can find the house?"

"I think I can."

"Okay, let's try it."

We were almost four hours later than the time that we had esti-mated we would meet Lourdes at the border in Juarez, and we were coming around the back way. There had been no possibility of mak-ing that meeting, especially after we had to take the extra time to enter Mexico. Now Felipe was excited that perhaps he would get to see his sister anyway. With Felipe's directions, Dave wandered through the development and drove up to the house thought to be Lourdes's. We went up to the door and knocked.

Lourdes came to the door and broke down crying. "We had given up seeing you. We waited and waited at the border and finally came home to eat. We were just sitting down to eat, and praying that God would somehow make a way for us to be able to see you—and here you are!"

We asked about all the people living in the frozen shacks on the outside road. Lourdes' husband who worked for the city, told us that it had been horrible, that the continuing freezing temperatures had put a strain on everything. There wasn't enough gas for people to heat their homes, if they even had that capability. Most people didn't have heat in their homes, and the poor people in the shacks had absolutely no protection from the cold. People were freezing to death. "We have been praying that we could find a way to help them," he said.

We told them that we had a trailer full of warm clothing. We told them about our plight at the border and then about looking for someone to help distribute the blankets and warm clothing. Lourdes was beside herself. "Oh, we can do it! We can go out first thing tomorrow and distribute everything to the people, it is an answer to our prayer!"

We unpacked everything and sorted all the clothing and items that might help those dangerously cold people. We had a little supper with their family and began our journey once again.

We talked all the way to our next stop. What if we hadn't been refused at Juarez? We would never have seen those shacks and all those people freezing to death. We would not have found Lourdes's house and been able to visit with Felipe's family or to provide them with the opportunity to help their desperate neighbors. And,we would have had a big problem trying to explain all those clothes and blankets for one family when we had to go through the 50 kilometer checkpoint still ahead of us. It seemed obvious to all of us that God had a purpose in our delay and our diversion.

᠙

CHAPTER XIII

GOD'S HAND...HIS SPIRIT...1996

I had made a promise to little José and to myself that day which I have been determined to fulfill: *"Yes, I will help you."*

José had been gone for several days, and when he finally returned he was alone, without his little sister Brianda or his little brother.

"Where have you been, José? We've missed you." José just smiled and gave a look with his large, almost black and slightly askew eyes. "Where's your little brother and sister?"

"They went on a trip with my mother and her friend in a truck," he said.

"Where are you staying, José?" I asked.

"With relatives."

It just seemed that something was wrong. "Well, José," I persisted, "I would like to see where you are staying. I would like to meet your relatives; could you take me there?"

What we saw as José took us to his "home" is beyond description. He was living alone in a dingy one-bedroom apartment located in a high-rise, low-cost housing development in Salagua. It looked abandoned. There was a dirty rag stuffed in the hole where a door handle should be—he was without lock or protection to keep out the unwanted.

As we entered, the stench was overwhelming; human and dog feces covered the floor. The urine-soaked mattress lay on the floor in the bedroom, uncovered, with cotton stuffing coming out of the holes made by rats nesting. We had to put a cloth over our noses, and even then we were close to gagging as we entered the different areas.

I hurried over to the broken window so I could gasp some fresh air before continuing. There was a little table in what used to be a kitchen. A candle that had been burnt down to a stub sat in the middle of the table with melted wax all over the table. The candle was obviously the only form of light at night, without electricity, running water, or any way to use the bathroom, except in the dead, broken, toilet bowl or on the floor. Living in the city dump would have been more sanitary and smelled much better.

José told us that he was staying alone during the times that his mother "traveled." He was so frightened at night and lay awake for hours, afraid because of the dark. He could hear people and noises outside the door, and he would imagine all kinds of danger, urinating in the bed because he was afraid of what might be in the dark waiting for him. The only food he had was the meal that he was able to get at the comedor.

I didn't realize that we were putting ourselves in a very illegal position and could have been accused of "kidnapping," but we couldn't leave José there, so we took him back to our home until we could find his mother. His head was full of lice, and we took him and a bar of soap to the outside shower, shampooing over and over. Then we sent him into the saltwater of the ocean trying to find a way to get rid of some of the lice and white nits that filled his black hair. He wore a pair of broken-down tennis shoes without socks, and when he took them off the smell was so bad, we put them out on the sea wall rather than in the trash to keep the smell out of the house.

José's mother never bothered to look for him. But he was our secret weapon to go back to the officials and beg for permission to open the casa hogar. We presented our petition again so that children like José could have a place to live, be cared for, and have food to eat. José lived with us in our home for six more weeks while the paperwork was being processed. He continued to wet the bed for most of those six weeks, but slowly he found a new security and began to believe that there were people who wanted to help him, and he was able to break the habit.

In June of 1996, after months of waiting, our paperwork was finally approved, and we had official permission to open the doors of "Casa Hogar Los Angelitos" and took in our first child...little José.

FINALLY OPEN

Our first location was lent to us. It was a retail building, located in downtown Santiago, with two pull-down metal garage doors for an entry. The upstairs was used for a dorm and the main level, which opened directly onto the street, was remodeled for kitchen, dining, and work areas. José Rodriquez and his wife Mari had just married, and they began their marriage as houseparents for the newly opened Casa Hogar Los Angelitos. Within a short time, we had twenty-four children coming from the local area of Manzanillo as well as communities throughout the state of Colima and even several hundred miles away from the states of Jalisco and Michoacán.

It was a terribly uncomfortable place for housing. When the "garage" doors were down, there was no ventilation on the lower level. The doors opened directly onto the sidewalk and street, so there was no yard or play area for the children. We put up a protection fence across the front openings to keep people and dogs from wandering in off the street and to keep the children from wandering *out* and onto the street. Hoping to build a real home for the children, we continued in this hot and uncomfortable place.

During the process of trying to get legal permission to open and operate a casa hogar, we discovered that we were the first casa hogar trying to open as a civil association (non-profit), and consequently the state of Colima didn't have laws or rules to establish the requirements to open a casa hogar as a civil association. Most casa hogars in the state of Colima were under the authority of the Catholic church.

Through our efforts to help little José, I had developed a good relationship with Lilia Delgado, who had been in a position of authority at the social services agency, DIF, in Manzanillo. The position she held was a three-year political appointment, and her three years had ended. I contacted Lilia, who came to work for us and began her first major project of writing and presenting to the state government proposed rules and regulations for establishing and operating a casa hogar under the legal authority of a civil association. These regulations were accepted, and we were approved as a legal entity.

One of the first cases we were involved with was a baby girl who was found crawling on the edge of the street where her teenage mother was living with the father of the child. The baby girl, Alma, was eight months old and weighed only eight pounds. She was suffering from extreme malnutrition and unable to eat or even take a bottle with a normal nipple when she was brought to us by DIF. For the first two weeks we cared for Alma, we fed her nutrients and sugar-water mixed with milk using a dropper. It took months of round-the-clock care to be sure whether she would survive.

In our second year, we were able to rent a second house and divided the children between the two properties, which were several miles apart. We made the properties work, but with more than 27 children now, we were outgrowing both of them and desperate to find better facilities.

Soon after opening the second house we were brought two little boys—Pancho, 4 years old, and his brother José, who was 5. Pancho and José had been found abandoned on an uninhabited farm...they would forage through the plants remaining that still had some produce, and eat whatever stale food they could find in the broken down shed they slept in. Their mother would leave them for days, alone to care for each other, while she "worked" the streets. Their little bellies were swollen from parasites and malnutrition and when they first came to live at the casa hogar we found that the two of them had developed a language of their own to communicate with each other.

Benjamin, José, Nancy, with Chema, Armando, Brianda, and Arturo; 1996

The first piece of property we were given to build on was part of a housing development. As part of the conditions of approval, the owner needed to set aside a certain amount of land for green space, schools, community benefit, or municipal or non-profit use. Casa Hogar Los Angelitos fit into the community benefit and non-profit category.

We cleaned the land, built a fence around the perimeter, and began the process of construction. I was concerned about the final documents, not knowing the laws of Mexican property ownership. With nothing but a contract in hand, I continued to ask about official title. "Don't worry, it is not a problem."

Well, we soon discovered it *was* a problem when we received word that the fence had been pulled up, the material storage shed had been burned down, and the land had been reclaimed.

One of our board members wrote a letter to the editor of the local newspaper criticizing the actions of the land owner. That night there was a knock at her door, and she found herself facing a gun and a threat that caused fear and retraction of her letter.

I cannot divulge more about this situation because of the risk of retaliation, but needless to say, we were set back in loss of funds, time, and energy.

Persevering, we found another beautiful piece of property that the owner was prepared to give to us *if* we bought the property next to it, which belonged to another family member. This time we made sure we had good, provable title to both pieces of property. We had our "primera piedra" (first stone) ceremony with the wife of the governor of the State of Colima as our guest speaker and honoring us by placing the first stone for this new project.

Our plans had been designed to house up to 1,000 children, including a small fruit tree and farming area, soccer field, area for vocational training, central area for administration, auditorium, clinic, and cafeteria. I don't know how I thought we were going to pay for all of this, but in blind faith, I moved forward, believing that God "owned all the gold and the cattle on a thousand hills," and surely He could provide the resources to take care of the orphaned children.

We began by building a road to the property and fencing the entire land.

When we bought the property connecting to the gifted property, there was a field of decorative, landscape palm trees planted on that property, hundreds of young trees. We were told that each tree was worth $300–$600 pesos, making our purchase one that could help pay for the initial construction of the property.

It was shocking when we discovered one morning that there had been a fire during the night, only on our property, burning all the palm trees and making them worthless. Even though we tried to hope that this fire had been an accident, a trash fire out of control, with the wind blowing in the direction of our palm trees, we knew that was not what happened. This was a blow to our hope for additional financial income. Not to be daunted, or lose faith, we continued with our preliminary work to begin actual construction.

In 1999, after driving from Colorado to Manzanillo with my mother and her husband Paul, we saw that something was seriously wrong with Paul. The doctors came and examined him, advising us that he was in the final stages of heart failure. I was calling the authorities with a medical service that we had, with the intention of flying him out of Mexico into a hospital in the states. Paul stopped me and said he didn't want to go, he knew he was dying, and he couldn't think of a more beautiful place to die than on the beaches of Manzanillo. It was only a day later that he passed away. We had each diligently stayed with him holding his hand and talking to him even when he couldn't respond.

Because of issues transporting a body across the border of Mexico, we made the decision to follow Paul's wishes for cremation, then we began the long journey back through ice and snow to the U.S. and Colorado carrying the container of ashes.

The first night in Guadalajara, I slipped and fell breaking my knee cap into three different parts, the pain was the most physically excruciating pain I had ever felt, but when some kind of doctor came and gave me a shot to help the pain and swelling, he thought it was a sprain, so not knowing what was really wrong, we continued on the road back.

I was in so much pain, I could hardly stand it, a fear and anxiety was beginning to overwhelm me.

When we arrived at my mother and Paul's home in Leadville, Colorado—which has an altitude of over 10,000 feet—I began to feel an intense pain building in my head that wouldn't subside, even with pain medication, it just continued to get worse.

Dave and I had begun the drive back to Vail and our home when I somehow realized I was in real trouble. Just before passing out I told Dave, "Get me to a doctor—hurry!" I don't remember anything after that. I was told that I would come to and each time ask, "Did someone die?" Then they would tell me, "Yes, Paul died." I would begin to sob until I would pass out again, then I would wake and ask again.

My life was once again spared. I was suffering from HACE (high-altitude cerebral edema), and I was told that if I had not received medical attention as quickly as I did, I probably would not have survived. My body was susceptible because of the emotional stress of Paul's death plus pain from an untreated break and then an extreme altitude change—from sea level to 10,000-feet-plus.

Death is never easy, even when it's expected. We each responded differently to that very personal experience, and my mother was once again a widow.

We returned to Mexico several weeks later. This time I was in a brace, and my mother was with us traveling alone.

We immediately began a capital campaign for funds to start construction and to drill a well for water. We received a contribution from a man from Minnesota for $10,000 U.S., sufficient to put in the 90-meter water well and pipe. Once we completed this well, we were prepared to begin the first building.

It was the next May, after Dave and I had returned to Colorado for a period of time with family, that I received a call from our attorney, Rafael de la Colina. "There's large dirt-moving equipment on the land. Are we in the process of construction? What is happening?"

"I have no idea," I said. "Please, let's quickly find out why men with heavy equipment are digging on our land."

After investigating at the city offices, we discovered that the state of Colima was building a huge drainage system to divert the flood-waters from the center area of the town of Salagua, and without warning, compensation, or even a letter to advise us, our property was one of the first that they confiscated to begin the 300-meter-wide ditch. This ditch was passing through the entire length of our long, triangular shaped property.

Our plans were crushed; it was impossible to build housing for children on each side of a huge and dangerous drainage ditch. Our plans were shattered. We could see the white pipe of the water well sticking out of one side of the ditch, now worthless.

It took us five years to get the compensation for the loss of this land and even then it was only the actual cost we had in the land. We were not compensated for the value of the land nor for the value of the loss. Once we received the "compensation" for our loss, we decided to purchase a small house close to the property that we had purchased during those five years of waiting. We moved the older boys into that property calling it *Casa 2*.

We made the two properties work, but with more than 27 children now we were outgrowing both of them, and desperate to find better facilities.

During that time, there were side issues that came up. People react differently to set backs and changes in the course of things. Some people lost confidence in us and the project, so they began to withhold support, financial as well as moral.

The man who contributed the $10,000 for the well demanded his money back with threats of retribution. We met him at a neutral location where we were meeting another group of people and gave him a personal check for the $10,000, since the funds he gave had been donated to the project and spent on the well. He tore up the check in front of the others but continued to harass us for the next year, making public threats and accusations.

It was another good learning experience: Now we don't accept contributions if there are strings attached or if we feel that the ulterior motive is not a positive and sincere one. We have had the opportunity to accept what appeared to be "laundered" money, which could have helped us to move forward financially. It also would have moved us into an illegal trap that we could never escape from.

This episode was not the last of the land "deceptions." We received a third piece of land, supposedly to help replace the loss of the previous piece of land. However, after beginning to build a wall and clearing the property, we discovered that there was a huge hole on the property, making it virtually impossible to build there without filling in the hole. We made a large "Clean fill dirt accepted" sign for the property and eventually the hole was filled. It took several years, but once again we were in the talking plans of construction—smaller this time, but a solid step forward.

Looking at a potential site with Lidia Rodriguez and Ramon Lopez

Felipe and I had gone to look at the property and to discuss the possibility of trading this property, which was now in a heavily developed area, for a much larger piece of property further outside of town. We looked at the land on January 5th. Dave flew into Manzanillo a couple of days later and surprisingly said he wanted to take a look at the land. So, we drove over, and, unbelievably, once again there were construction workers moving dirt, mixing concrete, and obviously doing some kind of construction. *What is going on*???

We stomped over to the person who appeared to be the boss. "This is our property. What are you doing on our property? Who gave you the right to be on our property?" He continued working and said, "I am working under the orders of the city. I don't know anything about who owns this property; you will have to go to the City and discuss it with them."

That was more than three years ago. We are still trying to resolve the issue. The mayor of the local area where the land was located had decided that they needed that land for a sports area, so they took it.

The city offered us several other pieces of property to take the place of the third piece that was taken away. One of the properties was ideally located, one block away from our existing building. As we began to move forward on receiving this property, a group of homeowners in the neighborhood began a campaign against us. "Don't give our land to foreigners!" They created such a noise that the city council (Cabildo) decided against transferring that property to Casa Hogar.

What good would it have done to try to explain to people who had their minds made up that Casa Hogar Los Angelitos was established as a Mexican Civil Association (non-profit)? That all the employees are Mexican; all the children are Mexican; all the property, assets, and permissions are part of the civil association; and no "foreigner" has ownership? What good does it do to try and talk to a group with a mob mentality?

CHAPTER XIV

There are two ways to live your life. One is as though nothing is a miracle.
The other is as though everything is a miracle.

Albert Einstein

YAÑIRA'S MIRACLE

When I first met Yañira, I was fascinated by her smile. She had almond-shaped eyes that lit up every time she smiled and cheeks that were so much rounder than her thin body should have produced. But it was her beautiful smile that made me want to reach out and hug her.

Yañira Desiree, abandoned before birth by a father who didn't even know she existed, was the firstborn of a young teenage girl who was living with one man and prostituting herself to many more over the following years.

Two more children were born, and it fell to Yañira to be the mother and homemaker. For days at a time, her mother would leave her alone to care for her younger brothers while their mother traveled with truckers who paid for her company or serviced mariners coming into the port on ships from around the world.

Sometimes there would be a "padrino" (stepfather) staying in the house; sometimes there was no one; so the door would be locked with Yañira and her little brothers inside for days at a time.

She never understood why her mother would become so frustrated and angry at her when she would return home from her trips. Her voice and slaps were like daggers in her heart. Yañira didn't realize that her mother was jealous, and it was fear that caused her to react in anger as she noticed her boyfriend watching Yañira's 14-year-old body more and more. Yañira only looked 11 or 12, she was so small and fragile. Her face was so fresh and so beautiful—she was a daily temptation to this man.

When no one was around, he would put his arm around her little frame, slip some pesos in her pocket and move his hand to her budding breasts. Where are the boundaries?

"Please don't! Please don't touch me!" She would scream inside her head. "What can I do?" She was shaking and quivering in fear. "What can I do?" It was tempting to take the pesos, if he would only touch just a little bit, not so much. She would twirl and turn away, trying not to make him angry as she moved her body away from his hands.

It was mid-morning that day, and "he" had finally left. Her little brother was crying from the beating he had received that morning while trying to defend his sister from that man, that monster his mother lived with, hands groping all over his sister—he couldn't stand to hear Yañira crying out, "Please stop, stop!" while struggling to get away.

"What can I do? What can I do?" Yañira decided at that moment to escape. Prying open the window and squeezing herself out through the small opening, after collecting the few coins she had saved from previous encounters, she began walking as fast as she could up the steep slope that led from her house to the highway above, and to what she hoped would be—freedom.

One flip flop was tearing loose at the toe, and the gravel on the side of the highway was embedding into the soles causing her to feel like she had rocks in her feet. But determined, she continued walking in the heat, with the cars whizzing past leaving their fumes and smells in her face. She would move from the gravel to the smoothness of the road when it was clear, thinking, "How much farther? Where am I going? What am I going to do?" Her lower lip would quiver in fear, and her tongue felt like it was growing twice the size. She kept swallowing to keep moisture in her mouth and kept moving.

Why? Why did her mother leave her alone with that man? Why had her father abandoned her? "What's wrong with me?" As she got closer to downtown Manzanillo and realized she had nowhere to go, no one to help her, she began to feel a sense of panic and nausea. She was so thirsty, pulling out the few pesos she had carried with her, she went into a little *deposito* by the side of the road and put the coins on the counter. "Un agua por favor." As she drank some of the water she tried to think, "Where can I go?"

DIF, the government office for helping the poor. That's it—she remembered going there with her mother to collect "dispensa."

"Please, Señora, can you tell me how to get to the office of DIF?"

The directions were simple: "Stay on the main road for approximately seven to eight kilometers, and you will see the sign on the building on your left just after you cross the railroad tracks."

Seven to eight kilometers? Her feet were dirty and sore from the eight kilometers she had already walked, and the strap on one sandal was loose. She was sweating from the heat, and her legs were feeling numb from the pace she had pushed herself to keep.

"Señora, what time is it?" Do I have enough time to get there before they close for the day? she asked herself. "Oh, dear God, please help me."

Yañira carefully replaced the cap, sticking the bottle into the little bag she had carried over her shoulder, and began the second half of her journey.

"Yañira, there are no orphanages, casa hogars, that will take you, you're too old. You are 14; 12 is the limit." Lilia Delgado, the social worker at DIF, felt sorry for this little girl who had walked so far in the heat and dust of the road to ask for help, but what could she do?

Yañira began to cry and pleaded, "What can I do, what can I do? Where can I go? Please help me."

"Perhaps, there is a possibility of help. You look much younger than your age. There is a casa hogar; if you tell them you are 12, they will take you in, and once you are there I am sure they will not send you away, even if they find out your real age. This casa hogar is in Santiago: Casa Hogar Los Angelitos. I will take you there."

Yañira had a dream—she had two dreams: she longed to know her father, and she longed to have her mother's love. It didn't seem that either dream would be fulfilled.

It was before her fifteenth birthday, her official quinceañera, that we discovered Yañira had leukemia. She had complained of pain in her stomach and when we took her to the doctor they found a lump, then the discovery of leukemia.

She took chemo shots twice a week and the days between the shots were just as difficult as the days of the shots—nausea and chills; she had perhaps two good days per week. Sometimes she was brave and smiled and tried to be positive; sometimes she said she wanted to die and wanted to cut her wrists hoping to end her pain.

We desperately looked for help to save this beautiful young woman. There was a new method that took the T cells and could somehow replace the bad with good. However, we had to come up with $75,000 pesos and find a match for her. The best match would be her father. But she had no idea who her father was or where he might be.

We looked for her mother's help but she wasn't interested. When we asked about the possibility of testing her younger brothers, we were told that wasn't possible and besides they had different fathers.

I put the word out trying to gather the funds together that would enable us to get her the transfusions. We made trips to Colima and then we began to make trips to Guadalajara, which is about a 4-hour drive from Manzanillo. Finally, we were sent to Mexico City where there was a doctor and hospital that seemed to have the capacity to do this procedure.

We had gathered several thousand dollars, but then ran into a problem because of an American woman, living in the area, who had decided she didn't believe that Yañira was really sick—she looked too good to be sick—and began to spread the rumor that Casa Hogar Los Angelitos was just using this story to try and get money. "It really isn't true," she would tell people. We kept running into closed doors and couldn't find additional funding.

In the meantime, Lilia Delgado, who now was working for us as a director of the casa hogar, began an intensive research through government agencies and old records to see if she could find the man who was Yañira's biological father.

The birth certificate had an address in Colima city at the time of her birth. That was a good start. Lilia then visited that address and found that the older couple living there had lived there for a number of years, and yes, they had a son that had moved to Culuacan in the northern part of Mexico, now married, with a daughter about 13 years old. Lilia explained the situation to this couple—who would prove to be Yañira's grandparents—and they contacted their son.

Yes, he had lived with a young woman for more than a year during that time, but had no idea that she might have had a child by him.

"Would you be willing to come to Colima to be tested to see if your DNA and blood type match? This is literally a life and death matter."

He came, and after having his blood type tested was convinced that he was Yañira's father. We were elated. We had a match, and he was willing to do whatever was necessary to save her life.

It is difficult for me as I remember this time and write these things down. For Yañira, it was a dream come true. Finally, she would know her father; finally she would belong. Even with the pain and difficulties, it was a good time for her.

We couldn't find the additional funds to pay the hospital, so my husband and I decided to pay the $4,500 difference. We gave the money to the hospital and began the process. We made at least four long trips back and forth to Mexico City for the preparations, sometimes staying in a hotel downtown close to the hospital and sometimes staying with a friend, Monica Welter.

It was during one of those trips that I contracted brucellosis, or as it's called in humans, undulant fever. A bacterial infection similar to malaria, it's caused by infected, unpasteurized cheese or milk, and like malaria, never leaves your body sometimes recurring if your immune system is low or you are under heavy stress.

We had set up a tentative time to begin some of the transplants. During those months, Yañira had been staying at our home in Manzanillo. We had hired people to be with her 24 hours per day whether we were in our home or not. Yañira was battling a secondary problem as well as leukemia—she had hepatitis B that had to be controlled in order for her to be a candidate for the transplant.

It was during the month of May that Yañira became very sick from the hepatitis. She was rushed to the emergency room in Manzanillo, but because her condition was so serious, they felt that she would need to be taken by ambulance to Guadalajara and then on to Mexico City.

She went into a coma, and the doctors didn't expect her to live.

I had gone back to Colorado, but when I received the news, I decided I needed to make arrangements to fly back down as soon as possible. I met Lupita Carbajal, who was volunteering with the casa hogar while attending college, and we flew directly to Mexico City and to the hospital where we found Yañira in what the doctors described as a coma and on life support.

Renting a room at a small hotel within walking distance of the hospital, we worked our way through the maze of the hospital, through security and into Yañira's room.

She was lying with tubes and life support hanging all over, connected to her frail little body, perfectly still and beautiful.

Sometimes we don't understand why we are led to do certain things, where the courage comes from, or the inspiration. Not knowing if it is inspiration or insanity. But, for some reason I spoke firmly and at the same time put my hand on Yañira's hand. "Yañira, I'm here. Lupita and I are here. We are here to tell you that it is not time for you to die, you need to wake up so that we can take you home and you can get better."

I don't know if it was the sound of my voice, the touch of my hand, or what. Yañira began to flick her eyelids and drowsily began to open them. For a brief minute, she seemed disoriented, and then she began to move her lips to say something. "I want to die."

"No, Yañira, it isn't time. Now, it is time for you to get stronger so we can take you home."

Yañira did get better, and we did take her home. She went to her school to see her favorite teachers and say hi to some of her friends. She visited the other kids at the casa hogar, and soon people began to talk about Yañira's miracle.

Yañira's father came from northern Mexico—Culuacan—bringing his wife and Yañira's younger sister who looked so much like Yañira that they could have been twins. It was a beautiful time for Yañira. Her new-found family spent time with her and made plans to return to Mexico City to begin the process for the transplant.

Everything was in place. We had deposited all the funds that the hospital required: $75,000 pesos to do the transplant.

By this time several months had passed, and for some reason the hospital kept putting off the transplant. They would check Yañira and then say, "We have to wait until she is better." Months went by, and Yañira was becoming weaker and weaker. She was having trouble walking and her strength seemed to be fading. We tried to persuade the hospital to go ahead with the transplant before things became worse, but the answer was always the same "We have to wait until she is better."

I had to go back to Colorado, trying to raise funds for the operation of the casa hogar and the completion of some of the remodeling that we were trying to finish on the property. Then the thing I feared most happened. Yañira once again had to be rushed to the hospital. This time, it was the social security hospital in Guadalajara. She had lost a tremendous amount of weight and had not been able to walk on her own for weeks.

As I write this and remember this beautiful young woman, it is difficult to hold back the tears. Alejandra, a lady who had been one of our housemothers, was staying with Yañira in the hospital.

The hospitals in Mexico are not like the hospitals in the U.S. A family member needs to stay with the patient to help care for the patient, or there is no one to help. Most of the time that person will sleep on the floor, or in a chair, and that is what Alejandra did. She had several pieces of cardboard that she put on the floor each night to sleep on, and a lightweight blanket that she smuggled into the hospital.

During that time, Yañira's mother began to come and stay for several days, relieving Alejandra. Although a painful and difficult time for Yañira, she was happy to finally have her mother reach out to her, sometimes even sleep next to her in the bed and hold her. It was the second part of her dream: to have her mother's love.

I was called again and told that Yañira was worse and that she was asking for me. I flew into Guadalajara and spent several days at her bedside, visiting with her about all the things she wanted to talk about. Talking about her new relationship with her mother, her father, her sister she had not known before, her boyfriend in Manzanillo, and all the other things that teenage girls like to talk about.

It was surprising how content she seemed while suffering so much. She said to me that all of her dreams had come true. She had met her father and had time to get to know him, and her mother seemed to truly care about her and love her.

I spent several days with Yañira and then took the bus from Guadalajara to Manzanillo to meet with the casa hogar staff and see the children at the casa hogar. I was scheduled to fly back out of Guadalajara on the afternoon of October 31, which only gave me a couple of days in Manzanillo.

Arrangements were made for Lupita to go back with me on the bus to Guadalajara to be with Yañira. We were scheduled to leave on the 5:00 A.M. ETN bus (a first-class bus line to Guadalajara).

Sometime between 3:30 and 4:00 A.M. of the morning we were to leave, a strange thing happened to me. I woke up to see a very large and beautiful being standing by my bed. For lack of a better explanation, I believe this "being" was an angel. At least, that is what immediately went through my mind. I was thinking at first, "This is the 'death' angel coming for me."

It feels strange to even talk about this or to expect anyone to believe what I experienced. However, as I was calmly thinking that the death angel was coming for me, I was assured by this same spiritual being that it was not me, but Yañira. I was being advised of what was to come.

Lupita spent the night at our house that night so she would be ready to go. I woke her up, we grabbed a sweet roll and a cup of coffee and headed out the door. As we rode the bus to Guadalajara, I tried to explain what had happened to me in the early hours of the morning. I told her to be prepared, because today Yañira would be taken home. I know Lupita didn't fully understand what I was saying at that time, or what I was trying to prepare her for, but everything would fall into place as the day went on.

We arrived at the hospital, and Yañira's mother was arguing with the hospital staff, "I want to get my daughter dressed and take her home where she belongs."

"Don't you know how sick she is? That's impossible!" they argued.

When I arrived, I told them, "Let her dress her daughter. It will be okay." Yañira wanted her nails painted and her now very short and thin hair fixed with *piojos* (little decorative wire hair clips that were referred to as "lice"). She was singing when Lupita and I arrived, and although she was being cleaned up after her uncontrollable bloody diarrhea had dirtied her sheet and hospital gown, she was smiling and singing.

Yañira with arms around Fernando and Selené,
children at the casa hogar

Lupita and I went to her bedside to let her know we were there. She asked Lupita to sing a song with her and to hold her hand. As she looked up at me, she said, "Nancy, this morning I had a special visitor."

"Who was that, Yañira?"

"A visitor who came and told me that there was a party being prepared for me—a big party, and I would be able to walk again. I could ride my bicycle, and the streets were made of gold. He told me that there was a beautiful sea of water and that everyone was waiting for me. That's why I want to look pretty, for my party." Then she looked at me and said, "Will you come to my party?"

I couldn't even talk because of the tears. I already knew. I am sure that the same visitor that had come to me in the early hours to warn me had come to Yañira to give her peace and comfort in her last hours. Yañira asked her mother to come and lie down by her for a few minutes and hold her. As her mother crawled into the bed, beside this little body that had become only skin and bones, she softly said, "I love you."

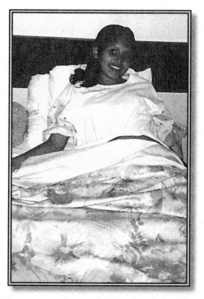

Yañira, at our home during her long illness

Yañira died that day, October 31, as I was flying out of Guadalajara. I knew when it happened. I felt it. She died with her mother snuggled beside her, and Lupita holding her hand, singing to her.

PART FIVE

God had brought their plot to nothing...all of us returned to the wall, everyone to his work...Those who built on the wall and those who carried burdens, loaded themselves so that with one hand they worked at construction and with the other held a weapon.

Nehemiah 4:15, 17

Now, when the rest of our enemies heard that I had rebuilt the wall, and that there were no breaks...they thought (conspired) to do me harm... they made false accusations and conspired to destroy me."

But Nehemiah answered "No such things as you say are being done, but you invent them in your heart...For they all were trying to make me afraid...."

Nehemiah 6:8-9

CHAPTER XV

LEGALISM, DETERMINATION, AND THOSE WHO PERSEVERE

After six years of trying to construct a larger facility, we decided to look for an existing property that would work for this project. In 2001 we were able to find a property that we felt would enable us to function efficiently, while providing a warm and home type environment for the children. It was an oasis in the middle of a desert.

As soon as we walked into the grounds we knew that this was a special place. The property had been in the family for a number of years and the owner who now lived in the U.S. wanted to sell the property at a cost that was less than 50% of the actual value.

I presented the proposal of the purchase of this building to the Scholten family saying that we could split the cost of the building and it could be a tremendous blessing for the work and for the children. The deal was made, the money was paid and we made plans to make the big move into what was now being called "The Hacienda."

Sometimes the appearance of success also breeds resentment and jealousies. That appeared to be the case in this situation. There were a few people who decided that this was too good for "those" children, and there were politically powerful people who wanted the property for their own projects, and intended to shut us down to get it.

O GOD, STRENGTHEN MY HANDS

April 1, I met with the mayor's wife for breakfast, offering help with the construction of a new area for the government social agency DIF, that she, as the Mayor's wife, was the president of. She had been to our home in Colorado by my invitation, as part of an effort to help raise awareness of the social issues involving children, and the need for financial help. When we met, she asked me about my mother who was suffering in the final stages of cancer. I had been gone for two weeks in February to be with my mother during her surgery, and had canceled an appointment with the mayor's wife. So, it was quite natural for her to ask, "How is your mother?"

I told her, "My mother is quite sick and asking for me to come home, so I have plans to leave on the 4th of April to be with her."

GO DIRECTLY TO JAIL—DO NOT PASS GO

"Nancy Neestrum? Guadalupe Carbajal?" they called out. It was late afternoon April 3 when two local police officers walked into the little administrative office where Lupita and I were going over the Casa Hogar books, preparing to pay bills for the week.

Lupita was handed an envelope, unsealed, with carefully folded papers. As she opened the papers, she looked at me and without knowing why, I felt this sense of panic that gripped my stomach. Then I was handed the same kind of envelope with the same carefully folded papers. I couldn't read the Spanish, I just saw my name written out in the introduction. Nancy Carolyn Walling Nystrom.

One of the officers smiled and said, "Out of courtesy to you, we will not take you today; however, you will need to meet with the judge Monday morning, and if you are not there you will be arrested." They turned around and walked out, leaving Lupita and me in a state of confusion. Lupita said we needed to call someone.

We called our attorney, Rafael, and he asked us to read the paper to him. Immediately he said, "Leave town, go by the back road. Go to Colima, find a motel that has a parking area that can't be seen from the road. Don't use the motel phone. Don't go out. Stay there until I can see the judge on Monday morning."

Lupita and I grabbed our purses and slipped out of town like frightened criminals. We now realized the seriousness behind these papers. We made it to the first *cuota* (toll booth) on the highway to Colima, and as I was paying the toll, the man in the toll booth told me that the Federal Police wanted me to pull over. My heart was pounding and I know Lupita's was as well. We were toast.

I told Lupita, "Try to be casual and your charming self. Whatever you do, don't show your fear."

The policeman walked over to us and leaned over to look into the window, "Buenos dias, señoritas." Of course, I am not a Señorita, but it is always meant as a compliment when you are obviously an older woman and you are referred to as a señorita. "Adonde va?"

Not knowing what to say, I decided the truth was best. "To Colima."

Then he said, "I noticed that you lost your hub cap as you were driving, and I wanted to give that to you." My hands were sweating, and I was sure that he could see my heart beating, but God gave us both the illusion of calm in front of him, and we gave our profound and sincere thanks and kept going with, "Thank you God, thank you God, thank you God!"

THE INDICTMENT

Throughout its history, Mexico has been under what we refer to as the "Napoleonic" laws, which basically work under the premise that "you are considered guilty until you can prove your innocence." As a result, it becomes very easy to make false accusations and *very* difficult to prove innocence, especially in some types of circumstances. These laws are now in the process of change, and a reversal of the Napoleonic laws will be put in place during the next several years. However, at that time, we were still operating under Napoleonic law.

We went through a series of false accusations, the worst of all crimes in the state of Colima. We were accused of allowing a volunteer to molest and rape a number of our girls. We were under indictment and the threat of imprisonment for over two years. For awhile, we had to go almost daily to the "big" jail where the judge and court were. Signing in and giving testimony over and over. Our girls had to go through the trauma of physical exams, but none of them were permitted to testify.

One of the most difficult things we have had to deal with throughout these many years has been finding the right people for this work. It is also the number one reason, besides funding, that orphanages and children's homes crumble from within: an employee entrusted with the care of children who turns out to be a fraud. We had one couple I refer to as the couple from hell; another man was sent by a church to help us open up the casa hogar whom I discovered was a pedophile. Thank God I discovered this before any children were brought into the casa hogar! It is a constant vigil. Today we have very strict rules and regulations that help to protect the children, the workers, and the casa hogar.

This time it was an unbelievable nightmare. But for me, it was a nightmare that became too real. Several of the mothers of the children were involved in questionable activities and entertainment.

There was a young U.S. volunteer who knew just enough Spanish to be sucked into some of the trap but not enough experience and maturity to realize what was happening. The list of players began with one of the house mothers who had (we later discovered) caused the same problem in another casa hogar, even though we had asked for references before hiring her. There were some powerful political figures who were willing to pay for a full-page news story/advertisement in the local papers to defame the casa hogar. As Dave refers to that time, "We were under siege."

Why would anyone make such a false accusation? In my mind it was unfathomable, but if they had been able to win, we would have had to close our doors, turn the property over to another agency, pay large sums of money to the families of the "victims," and go to jail—that simple.

I was under "house arrest" and couldn't leave the country without permission of the court. If I did leave, I would have lost my right to ever return.

I was finally able to get permission from the judge to make an emergency trip to Houston where my mother was hospitalized in the last stages of cancer. I got permission on April 16 to leave and was scheduled to take the 1 A.M. bus from Manzanillo to Guadalajara then fly from there to Houston on the seventeenth.

As I was getting ready to leave the house to catch that bus, the phone rang. It was my sister-in-law calling to tell me that my mother had just passed away. I was devastated, and even to this day have a difficult time trying to forget my anger and to forgive those who were involved in this horrendous delay. I arrived home in time for the funeral.

My family and friends said to me, "Give up. It will never work. Walk away!" But I thought of the children. I thought about Pilar, Arturo, Benjamin, and the others. What would happen to them? They had no other safe place to go. Even with the threat of jail, I couldn't walk away.

During difficult times, we have had various people who probably have not had much experience working in foreign countries ask me questions such as, "Why do people dislike you so much that they would try to destroy you?" Or perhaps they would make statements such as, "If this were meant to be, if this were God's plan, it wouldn't be so difficult." However, I believe that life itself is challenging, so does that mean we are not to live it or that we will not have obstacles and challenges? In studying the great prophets and heroes of the Bible—God's people—I did not find even one of them that didn't have some combination of setbacks, challenges, fears, criticism, and efforts to sabotage their work by others. There were failures, misunderstandings...some were thrown in jail, some suffered discouragement, some had to overcome bad decisions—but all had to ultimately depend on God for their strength and had to be willing to stand firm in their faith.

Statements like these and other criticisms that I felt were unfounded pushed me to constantly re-examine myself and the situation and to look inside my own agenda to challenge my own faith. However, I did not find these statements to be biblically founded and had to encourage myself to overcome and look past these criticisms. These challenges to my life and faith actually strengthened my personal relationship with Jesus Christ and my faith in God's faithfulness.

I have a card that I received not too long after my mother died, a very difficult time. It was a funny card, but perhaps had just enough truth in it that I have kept it all these years. It says, "Difficult times are God's way of teaching us how to deal with adversity. In the old days, He would have just sent us a plague of locusts!"

It has been crucial that I set my mind to the purpose and, to use a quote from Theodore Roosevelt, "Speak softly and carry a big stick." My big stick is my unwavering faith in God and His power to accomplish this vision.

STAND FIRM, BE STRONG

Your source of power is Almighty God.
Don't Touch My Anointed

It was during that difficult time that the words came to my heart: "If you believe that I am God, and this is My work, then by faith, you must stand firm—just stand—and trust Me to do what you cannot."

Lupita Carbajal, who was now the Administrator of Casa Hogar, was under the same attack and indictment as I was. She was still living at our house in Manzanillo as a security measure. We were not going via road to the casa hogar but trying to take care of everything we needed to do by phone or asking people to come to us. We were subject to arrest if we left the house at that time. Lupita and I met to discuss our next step, and after I told Lupita what I felt was our instruction, we made the commitment to stand firm, hold onto our faith, and wait for God.

Things did begin to change. When these accusations came up, a number of the children were taken away from our care. We lost all but seven of the children. Some of the children were put back on the streets or with the abusive families that they had been taken away from. I was so concerned about each child who was lost to us and secondarily concerned about the future of the casa hogar if all the children were taken.

I told Lupita that we must find a way to bring in more children. We would not even be considered a legitimate casa hogar with only seven children. We could possibly be shut down, which, of course, is what the ultimate goal was for some of the people involved.

I told Lupita that I felt we needed at least fifteen children to be functional. Within several days of that statement, Lupita received a call from a state organization, the "Asistencia Privada" in Colima. They had five children in terrible need from the area of Tecoman.

Would Casa Hogar Los Angelitos be able to take them? *Yes! Yes!* We would be extremely happy to take them.

LUPITA CARBAJAL AND THE LEPE FAMILY

Lift us up so we can see beyond the confines of the things that limit our view.
                    Father Greg Boyle, **Tattoos on the Heart**

Lupita had become my right hand in the work with the casa hogar. Even though she had been raised on a remote ranch in the hills of Manzanillo, she had become determined to continue her education. In elementary school, she would walk the dirt road that took her from the "ranch" down to the little town 45 minutes below named Chan Diablo. When it was time to attend junior high (secondary) and high school, she found a relative in town who would let her live with them so she could continue. In college she had specialized in two areas of study, Social Work and Administration. To accomplish the things that she accomplished was unusual for children growing up in similar circumstances and she had to be determined and strong.

The situation and family that began to turn things back around was handled by Lupita. The following is her report.

> After attending a reunion for the Junta de Asistencia Privada of the state of Colima, the director, Sra Alejandra reported the situation of a family with five members that were minors, in a situation of poverty and abandonment, originally from Tecoman, Colima.
>
> On 23 October, I visited the home of the Lepe family. I found a very humble place, filled with eleven family members, seven minor children and four adults: the father, aunt, grandmother, and great-grandmother.
>
> The economical sustenance was provided by the father and aunt. The grandmother was blind, and the great-grandmother was physically incapacitated.
>
> I interviewed, on behalf of Casa Hogar Los Angelitos, the father, Sr. Raúl Lepe Hernández, to form a plan of help for his five children.

The children proved to be in a dysfunctional situation, abandoned by the mother who left for a relationship with another person. The father had the legal rights for the five minor children and was responsible for their care. He worked in a restaurant on the beach and left the children in the care of the grandmother and great grandmother, both physically incapacitated.

The Lepe case was a special case needing urgent intervention because of the health of the children and the physical conditions they were living in. So on October 23, all five children and their father were transported to the Casa Hogar Los Angelitos facilities. When they entered the casa hogar, they were surprised and wanted to investigate all of the places. In a short time, they seemed to feel confidence and the two little boys began doing cartwheels on the grass.

The children were taken to the health clinic for medical examinations. They all were suffering from malnutrition, parasite infestation, and were extremely dirty. The doctor even asked that the children be taken back to the casa hogar and bathed then brought back to the clinic for further tests.

The children and the father were taken into the dining area to be fed. The cook reported that the five children and their father ate a total of forty tacos before they stopped eating. It was obvious that they had not had much food to eat for quite awhile.

All of the children were sent to shower and wash their hair and body with lice shampoo, and then they were all sat down in order to interview them and their father. Brenda, the oldest girl, was approximately eight years old. She was separated from the rest of the children by her father, and he asked her about going into the casa hogar. Brenda began to cry, but at the same time started nodding her head up and down for yes.

The second day, when the children were taken back to the doctor, it was discovered that both Francisco and little Raúl had fairly high temperatures. After several tests were made, it was discovered that both little boys had *dengue hemorragia* (hemorrhagic dengue). Within several hours, little Raúl had started bleeding from the dengue, and then Francisco. They were taken to the hospital, and treatment began immediately, taking several days to get the bleeding under control.

The father visited the boys constantly during their hospitalization, bringing something each time—milk, cookies, juice, etc.

The first few weeks of adaptation at the casa hogar is difficult for every child who comes in, but it was especially difficult for the Lepe children, who were shy and exhibited a great deal of depression and anger. Francisco, who was six years old, would take every opportunity to express his anger by climbing up on the roof, throwing rocks at any and everything, and waiting close to the entrance gate hoping his father would come back.

Brenda refused to eat and spent much of her time in her bed embracing her pillow and a small doll that had been given to her when she arrived, crying most of the time. When asked, "What's wrong, does something hurt?" she would only shake her head back and forth to say no. She didn't want to talk to anyone for several weeks, then said, "I miss my mother so much."

Graciela and Laura never mentioned or asked for their mother and seemed to adapt much faster. They soon learned to love having their photos taken, posing at every opportunity. Little Francisco and Raúl recovered quickly from dengue and malnutrition and in a few weeks began to gain weight and recuperate.

A couple of days after the Lepe children arrived, two more children came, and then another, and soon we were receiving children five at a time.

Although a number of people from the foreign community and local Mexican community had turned their backs on us and shunned us for a period, not wanting to be associated with a possible corruption charge, there were courageous people who began to come forward. One of those couples were the Stouts from Iowa. New to our project, they came over one day and said, "We are here, and we will stay as long as you need us. We believe that people need to think about the children."

With their influence in the foreign community, more people began to slowly come forward to help. Eventually (more than two years later) our legal situation cleared up, and we were totally cleared of all accusations.

The saddest part of the story is what happened to the children who were taken away during this time. Many have come back to visit. Most of the girls had moved into a relationship and had a least one baby before they were 13 or 14 years old. Most had not been able to continue with their education, and I can only imagine what some of the others have been through.

Throughout the years, we still have had to deal with gossip and other difficult circumstances, but we have been able to rescue and care for hundreds of children. When we first began with the comedors, people in the Mexican community accused us of taking the children to Canada and selling them or their organs.

When we tried to get the legal permissions to open the doors to the casa hogar, we were accused of being a cult wanting to brainwash the children or proselytizing them. When we were going to receive a piece of land within two blocks of the casa hogar—land that the city was going to use to replace the piece of land that had been taken away from us—a large group of the neighbors came to the council meeting with big signs, putting an article in the newspaper that said, "Don't give our land to foreigners!"

When you see the children in our project, you will not see bloated stomachs, emaciated bodies, or matted hair filled with lice. You will see beautiful, happy, well-fed and cared-for children. However, that is not the way they came to us. Our children come from situations of abandonment, abuse, and extreme poverty. We have to go through the process of "de-licing" them, medicating them for amebic and worm infestations, and work to correct the malnutrition that most suffer from.

Many of the children we began caring for came with little or no formal education. Some have learning disabilities and emotional trauma because of the life they were subjected to. So we tutor the children in order for them to enter public school. Teachers didn't always want to accept our children, saying, "They are street kids; they can't even do the work." Over and over we have proved them wrong.

In these years, we have seen so many stories first-hand. One little boy was only four years old, living in a *palapa*, and was passed from person to person to care for him. He learned to hop on the local bus and ride as far as it would take him and then return again. When we found him, he was tied to a post like a dog in order to keep him from running away while his drunken grandfather was passed out in a hammock. He was kicking away the mice that wanted to gnaw at his little feet and was nothing more than skin and bones, suffering from extreme malnutrition.

During his first few years in the casa hogar, we didn't think we would be able to keep him. He was like a wild animal, climbing on the roof, the walls, running from everyone, or digging his heels in the ground to keep from being moved. It took patience and determination to make the changes needed in his life. Today, he is one of the smartest students in school, an unbelievable artist, and seems to have the ability to quickly learn anything that he sets his mind to. He is a star in my book of life.

I realized during the early years of this work that providing nutrition for hungry children was life-saving and important. Empty stomachs need to be filled. However, we needed to be able to provide more. It became clear that children could not move out of the devastation of extreme poverty and hopelessness and break that cycle without education, economic opportunity, and hope for the future.

No child chooses to be born in poverty, but as it has been shown, "children learn what they live." If poverty and abuse is all they know, that is all they expect and what they repeat. I knew that we needed to do more than to rescue children and fill their stomachs. We needed to fill their hearts and their minds as well. We needed to be able to change these children's lives, give them choices, self-esteem, tools for success, and dreams to build a future.

During the early years of the casa hogar, we didn't have special staff to tutor the children. It was during that time that I noticed some of the children didn't want to go to school and had that look of shame when they were asked why.

Finally, we discovered the root of the problem for them. Most of them were behind in school or a little older than the others in class. There would be children, and even some teachers, who would laugh and refer to them as "those burros" or "donkeys from the casa hogar." I was furious and heartbroken for the children at the same time. How ignorant can people be?

It was then I made a decision to do things differently. We would rescue children, nourish them, give them medical attention, and care. Then we would provide spiritual and moral guidance *and* develop a program that would enable them to meet the standards of the education system and help them to excel. *We would educate the children.*

We now have tutors as part of our staff and provide special programs that help our children learn the skills they need to become successful, self-confident young people, proud of who they are so that they will never feel ashamed or inferior to other children. Today most of our children maintain a grade-point average of 8.5 or higher (based on a scale of 10). Many of them place first in their classes rather than last, and they all are proud to say, "I am from Casa Hogar Los Angelitos!"

After a child has been with the casa hogar for a period of time, their lives *and* their dreams change. They begin to believe in the future and to see their own potential.

Sometimes, young girls come into the casa hogar with a desire to be like their mother or sister, thinking that they might become a "table dancer" or "entertainer" in a "botanero" or bar. Sometimes it takes a year or more before those goals begin to change, and they start to see other options for their lives—to realize that there are other careers possible for them.

Without solid education, it is impossible to break the cycle of poverty.

RODRIGO AND ALBERTO

Rodrigo and his brother Alberto came to us when they were seven and nine. Their mother had abandoned them, leaving them with a father who was abusive, drinking to ease the pain of his anger and frustration with the hopelessness of his life. He went out on the fishing boats and hired out when there was work, drinking when there wasn't. Without education, he was unable to find better or more consistent work.

The boys would walk the streets looking for their mother, never believing that she couldn't be found somewhere if they looked hard enough. Jumping on one of the buses, they would persuade the drivers to give them free rides to areas where they thought she might have gone. Then, disappointed, they began the journey back to their very impoverished home. There were many nights when they slept on the streets, covering themselves in the night with newspapers left in the trash or with cardboard they might find behind the stores. When they made their way back to their father, his fury would manifest itself with beatings and yelling.

Rodrigo has said, "I never thought of myself and my brother as being 'street kids.' We were just looking for our mother."

One day, after Rodrigo had been at the casa hogar for almost three years, he was in the reception area sitting behind the desk when I came in, sitting down across from him to talk with him a little. I put my reading glasses down on the desk, and Rodrigo picked them up, put them on, and feigned a very sophisticated look on his face while pretending to give me instructions.

I laughed and asked him, "Rodrigo, do you want to be a teacher when you grow up?"

He replied, "No."

I was sure that I had discovered his life dream, so I asked again. "You don't want to be a teacher when you grow up?"

"No," he said.

"Well then, what *do* you want to be when you grow up?"

He looked at me and said, very matter-of-factly, "I want to be President of Mexico."

They say that if you dream it, you can accomplish it. Rodrigo's dream had begun to develop.

LITTLE GABRIEL

Little Gabriel was crying in pain, barely able to breathe as he tried to straighten the vegetables he was responsible for selling. The long cuts on his back were beginning to bleed even more as his body throbbed in its effort to regain equilibrium. His "padrino" had left in a tirade of angry threats after beating Gabriel with the rusted electrical wire that he had found on the side of the road. "Lazy, worthless little..."

Gabriel was only nine years old. His slight frame was thin from lack of nutrition. Wearing only a loose pair of pull-on shorts, he had no protection from the attack. He had tried to sell more, had tried to be careful, had tried to please, but nothing seemed to please.

As he tried to set the three-wheel "vendors" bike upright, looking around to make sure the man wasn't returning, he sat down on the side of the road.

His plight was being observed by a restaurant owner. Afraid to get involved, she was relieved when Lupita Carbajal came in for a fast lunch before heading back to the casa hogar. "Lupita, you have to do something. This little boy was just brutally beaten by his stepfather with a metal electric wire. See how he is bleeding. We have to call someone before that man comes back!"

Interfering with family or other altercations could have very serious repercussions and open the door for revenge later. However, Lupita had spent her childhood growing up on a ranch in the mountains, out of Manzanillo, learning to be careful in order to survive but to fear nothing. She immediately called the Red Cross and then the local police. They took little Gabriel into the restaurant to clean the blood off his back and put antiseptic ointment and gauze onto the already swelling, broken slashes on his skin.

The police were waiting for the stepfather when he returned, hauling him off in the back of their pick up, taking him to jail for child abuse. Little Gabriel was taken to the casa hogar to be cared for while he was healing. Gabriel lived in the casa hogar for over a year, and during that time he was re-enrolled in school and getting his body built up with proper nutrition.

His stepfather was, of course, "appropriately" contrite, pleading that he had learned his lesson, and he was released from jail after only several weeks with a strong reprimand from the judge, warning him against ever abusing any child again. He and Gabriel's mother eventually petitioned to regain custody, and sadly we said goodbye to our little Gabriel.

Saying goodbye to one of our children, even if under the best of circumstances is the very hardest thing I do. And we never know when we say good bye which direction that young life will take. All we know is that we gave that child a time of love and acceptance, a different look at themselves and of the possibilities in life.

Little Gabriel is no longer little—he is a tall, handsome young man who took the time to re-introduce himself to Lupita this past year and to thank her for rescuing him.

CHAPTER XVI

Though you give all your goods to feed the poor and have not love, it is nothing.
1 Corinthians 13 (paraphrased)

I met Dr. Guiber Nuñez just after he set up his medical practice in Manzanillo in 2001. He was a young man from Guerrero who had completed his internship at the Social Security hospital in Manzanillo, where he met and fell in love with beautiful Emilia, Lupita's sister. I was sick, and Lupita took me to see him. His small office was set up in a building that was old and hard to find. Perhaps he had one or two patients per day at the most. I immediately fell in love with the gentleness of Guiber's spirit.

Guiber's father left when Guiber's mother was pregnant with his younger sister, leaving them alone to look for help from her family. So, Guiber's mother, Guiber, and his soon-to-be-born little sister moved in with his grandparents in the mountain town of Tecoanapa, Guerrero.

Guiber's grandfather had traveled back and forth to the U.S. during the forties and fifties working on farms in California. During that time, he was converted to Protestant Christianity and began worshiping at a local Spanish-speaking Evangelical Presbyterian Church. When he returned to Guerrero, he helped establish a small Presbyterian church in his community, preaching sometimes, and training his family in the spiritual concepts of this faith. He worked six, many times seven hard days each week during the season, walking each day to the hot cane fields in his home area of Tecoanapa to provide for his family.

The cane had to be chopped by hand using a sharpened machete, one cane at a time, then tied and piled in stacks, loaded on wagons pulled by burros, and taken into the local warehouse to be sold for pennies (*centavos*). The real profit would be made by others—after the canes were processed and sold to retailers. As a laborer in these fields, your pay was determined by the number of "piles" you were able to complete.

The work was brutally hot, with heat sometimes in the 90s and 100s. Accidents from the sharp knives were a daily occurrence. While working or walking, you always had to be aware of the poisonous scorpion sting or the tarantula that loved to live among the leaves of the corn, the sugar cane plants, and the banana trees. Gloves were never used, so a man who worked the fields had hands that were leathery and calloused matching their worn and sun weathered faces. A woman or child's more delicate hands were the same. The basic leather sandals—*huaraches*—were little protection from the insects, cuts, bruises, and unforgiving hot soil.

In the "wet" months of July, August, September, and October, the real threat was the malaria, the cholera from contaminated water, and the dengue that was spread by infected mosquitoes.

This was the life that Guiber knew: working the fields, welding a machete with his grandfather, studying during the week, and learning the scriptures at his grandfather's feet.

Our youngest son Rob had spent a year between his college studies to help us open and operate a new idea in Manzanillo—a cyber café. This project was opened with the idea that it would be an income-producing operation and provide an office for our administration as well as a place for public awareness for the casa hogar project. We were looking at renting out a small office space in the cyber café, and I offered Guiber the possibility of moving his office in with us, which I felt would provide him a more prominent location for his practice.

Guiber remodeled and moved into the cyber café office space and began to receive patients. However, within a few months, we had to make a sudden change. The building rent had increased, and we were not making enough profit to make it worthwhile to keep it open. A new area had been built on the casa hogar site that was intended to be used for offices and a small clinic, giving us the opportunity to move everything into one location. So we made the decision to close the cyber café.

However, one problem: poor Guiber had just remodeled his area in the cyber café because of my encouragement, and we were now going to have to ask him to move again. Obviously disappointed, "I just finished the remodel," he said, "putting all the extra cash I had into this potential. Now what?"

I began to present another option. "Well, Guiber, I know it seems that this is an inconvenience, and you are disappointed. However, I want to make another offer and hope it will work for you and will help to make this difficult situation right. We have built a little clinic as part of our new construction at the casa hogar. I know the location is a little out of the way, but I believe that God will bless you if you join with us by providing medical attention for our children. At the same time, you could still have your private practice in the office."

Actually, the casa hogar is located in an area that is only one block long, and it's difficult to find even if you are looking for it, so I really didn't think that Guiber would consider this offer.

To my surprise Guiber hesitantly responded, "What are my options? I've put all my savings into remodeling this location, and I don't know how it would work at the location you have, but this morning I was reminded of the scripture, 'Put first the Kingdom of God, and all these things will be added unto you,' and for some reason I believe that God's hand might be in this—and what more do I have to lose?"

Guiber moved all of his equipment and set up his medical office in the casa hogar, preparing for his first day. He assumed that it would be similar to his days at the two previous locations—5 to 6 patients per day, with the opportunity to build his practice.

He arrived at 10 A.M. for his first day, and in his own words, "I couldn't believe that Nancy could be having a party at the casa hogar on the first day my office was to be open, inviting all these people—and using part of my reception area. Who *were* all these people?!"

What a surprise when Guiber was told they were all patients waiting to see him—close to forty people. Many had been waiting for more than an hour. That was the beginning of God's blessing and Guiber's relationship with the casa hogar.

During the first year that Guiber worked with the casa hogar, he was working several jobs to make ends meet and provide for his wife and small daughter. However, his private practice flourished as he gained a reputation within the community, giving him the opportunity to quit the extra jobs and concentrate on his private practice.

Although Guiber was becoming successful, he wasn't content. He began talking to me about the horrible poverty and desperation of so many of the people in his home state of Guerrero, one of the poorest states in Mexico. He felt fortunate because he had been able to go to school to become a doctor when in his home, only 3% of the population ever completed high school and college. He told me how hard the people worked, many in the fields or laboriously picking, deseeding, and cleaning the little wild hibiscus flower called *jamaica*.

Because they didn't have the means to take their crops to a large market, they had to sell for close to nothing. Many traveled from their homes to Mexican states further north to work the fields during the season, living under plastic covers, sleeping on the cold ground at night, and working twelve to fourteen hours every day in the hot sun.

Guiber had promised himself that if he became successful, he wanted to find a way to help his people, the people of Guerrero.

With Guiber's commitment to help his people, we made the decision to bring food, supplies, medicines, and other needed relief for the people of Guerrero in the region of Guiber's home town.

It's a fourteen-hour drive from Manzanillo to Guerrero. There are two basic ways to make that trip by car: down the beautiful but isolated and dangerous coast through Michoacán and Guerrero, past the city of Acapulco, and then west into the mountains of Guerrero. The other route is longer but safer: the toll road through Guadalajara, Tuluca, and Mexico City, then west toward the entry into the Costa Chica area, turning onto the long two-lane road that takes you into the mountainous area.

After spending the night in Guadalajara and purchasing a carload of bulk food, plastic bags to separate it into, and a record book, we headed toward Mexico City on the toll road.

When we finally arrived at Guiber's home they were waiting for us with *posolé* (a traditional type of soup made from grains of corn that had been soaked overnight in lye water until it puffed into something that looked like a soft chewed gumball, combined with pork and garnished with chilies, onions, lettuce or cabbage, and cilantro), homemade corn tortillas, and about ten other family members.

Guiber's grandfather's house was fairly large compared to other houses in the area. A two-story, unpretentious concrete hacienda-style house with a long covered veranda where several straight-back chairs waited. A large bag of corn that had been shucked and the kernels put aside to grind for tortillas sat on the veranda. Guiber's grandfather had saved the money he earned during his years as a farm laborer in the United States and built his house, little by little, each year as he returned home.

As was typical in traditional Mexican families, everything was modest—straight-backed chairs lined up against the walls, and there was minimal decorations. The bathroom, next to the kitchen, had a light shower curtain that you could pull almost closed if you went in, but it was smart to keep an eye on that area if you were thinking of using the bathroom, and advise someone you were going in, since it was difficult to tell, other than by noises, whether someone was already there.

Plumbing seems to be a problem all over Mexico. Toilets never have a seat on them; toilet paper is scarce, and sometimes, even if there is a tank, you have to pour a bucket of water into the toilet to flush it.

We found our rooms upstairs in the still-waiting-to-be-finished "extra" bedrooms and settled in for the night. Lupita and I were in one room, watching for the spiders that we had seen working their way around the room and aware that everyone who walked by the room could see in because everything was pretty open.

The next morning, after discreetly dressing while watching the open door and windows, I chose not to shower. I would have had to use the little hose that brought the cold water into the very small bathroom area for a quick wash and then fill up the bucket for the toilet. However, necessity required that I use the bucket, which I thought would never fill up with the small stream of water that came out of the hose.

One of the other things you learn, if you travel into various parts of Mexico, especially in the more natural areas, is to keep your shoes on at all times, unless you are in bed. Then make sure you shake them out before putting them on to prevent unwanted creeping visitors from hiding there. Scorpions and tarantulas love the warmth of unoccupied shoes in the night.

We had a quick breakfast of eggs, tortillas, chilies, and instant Nescafé, and then we were taken to the front veranda where about twenty people had congregated.

We began trying to explain the food program and the system that we were hoping to set up in the local area, looking for volunteers to continue to work. People looked at me as if they could not believe what they were hearing, "Como?" How can we begin this?

It took about an hour of discussion, and I decided to tell a story from the Old Testament to these sincere and humble people as a closing inspiration. When it was time for the "Children of Israel" to cross the Jordan River into the "promised" land, the river was raging with floods and seemed impossible to cross. The messenger of the Lord told Joshua that the priests were to carry the ark and go before the people, crossing the river first, and as soon as the priests step into the water, the river will open up for the people to cross over.

I said, "To accomplish the impossible, you must have the faith to "step into the water," and that is what we are going to do."

Later that day, we made a treacherous drive along a mountain road with ruts and rocks that had to be carefully avoided to prevent sliding or bouncing over the edge of the road and down into a gully. We climbed for approximately forty-five minutes until finally reaching the little pueblo of El Charco. Here we unpacked the food, clothing, medical supplies, and reading glasses that we had brought.

People lined up as Dr. Guiber—who had served this town several years before during his social services program—began to give examinations, dispense medicines, and pass out the reading glasses. After hours of attending one person after the other, we were invited to a family's house for dinner.

By this time, we were hungry and anxious to have some food. On our path to the home we had been invited to for dinner, Lupita and I realized that we had about 10–12 young teen boys following us, lagging behind closely enough to stay with us but not too close. So we surprised them by stopping abruptly and talking with them for a few minutes.

They were at first shy, hanging back, and seemed afraid to talk, not sure how to handle this situation. Then, as we started joking with then, they began to slowly respond with us. One of the questions we asked, which is a typical question you ask around young teens when you don't know what else to ask, was "What are your dreams for the future?"

The boys hesitated, looked at each other, and then several of them said, "We want to go to school." The one-room school they had only went to the 5th grade, if the teacher couldn't make it up the washed out road during the rainy season, or was sick, there was no school. It was impossible for any of the children to be able to go back and forth to the town below to continue their education, and because this was an extremely poor mountain community they certainly would not have the funds to pay for room and board in order to live with a family in town.

Lupita and I both felt so sad for those boys and the bleakness of their future. They were stuck. We began to ask ourselves, "How can we help?" It was from this encounter that we decided to open the doors of the casa hogar for a limited number of poor children, who had no other options, for the sole purpose of continuing education.

We continued on our walk for dinner. Others joined the group, each wanting to be part of this oddity of people, to socialize and listen to the conversations. Finally, after an extensive "on-going" prayer of thanks, dinner was served. We had a lukewarm drink similar to tea, although I am not sure what it really was, and each person received two to three pieces of graham crackers. It was very humbling to think that this family had shared what little they had with us, without complaint, embarrassment, or apologies. A cup of tea and three graham crackers.

During the years that followed the program in Guerrero, "Ministerios de Amor" (Ministries of Love) became a program of relief and help to local communities in the hills outside Manzanillo as well. The lack of educational opportunity we saw in Guerrero also encouraged us to open our doors for youth from places such as Guerrero who lived in extreme poverty. At the casa hogar, they can continue their education.

> He who serves the poor serves God.
>   Gandhi

Nancy with Lupita Carbajal and Dr. Guiber Nuñez in Guadalajara on that first trip to Tecoanapa

During these years, people have come forward from all areas to meet each need—sometimes at the ultimate moment, sometimes a lot later, and many times different from what I thought I wanted, but always the need has been met. When we needed legal help, a local attorney came forward and gave his services for eight years without charge. Our architect drafted plans and designs and gave advice for over twelve years without fees.

We continue to have dedicated workers who believe in the vision and the mission and who give from their hearts for these children. Volunteers have come and given their time and energy throughout these years. Different churches and organizations have taken the vision and commitment to make a difference in children's lives.

When I think of the words that I first heard—"Feed My Children"—I realize that those words were not just about food for the stomach — they were also about food for the heart, soul, spirit, and lives of these precious children. When a child cries out in anguish, it is sadness for the entire world. When a child cries out in joy, it is a joy that fills all of heaven.

Often we become so busy, so involved in the business of life that our spirit is closed and unreceptive. After my son died, my spirit was open, tender, and seeking God's voice and comfort. I never had any desire or thought of opening a food kitchen, or a children's home, or becoming an advocate for abused and abandoned children. But God saw something else in His plan for me—something much different from the plan that I had designed for myself back at West Fourteenth Avenue Baptist Church.

Carrying in the bags of rice and beans for the people of Tecoanapa, Guerrero

I believe the vision that God put in my heart—to provide hope for desperate children—is without limit, because God is without limit. He is the father to the fatherless, and He can open doors that no man could have opened. Children who have no hope can begin to hope.

Children who have no future can have a future; children whose lives will be changed can change those around them, change their communities, change their country, and change the world they live in.

We face daily challenges that, at times, seem overwhelming. Yet this vision continues to grow. Programs and people continue to be put into place that will create a solid base, provide the foundation and opportunity for unlimited growth, and enable us to reach thousands of children in the future.

Mothers and children in Guerrero, lined up to receive food

The accomplishments and events of these past years have not removed the pain in my heart. The loss of my son will always be there; yet, I see the faces of all the children that we have rescued, clothed, fed, and cared for, whose lives have been changed, and who are as close to my heart as if they were my own children. When I realize that these feet truly have been able to bring hope and peace to children who had no hope, then I find peace and comfort, even in loss.

The grief, the prayers, God's message, the children, and this very interesting key changed my life and those lives around me. My life continues to change as each day brings its portion of good and difficult and as I have seen others whose lives are changed forever.

I believe we all have a mission and purpose—a calling—for our lives. The vision and mission that I carry in my heart was manifested as a result of my son's death. There may be those who say the visions and the voices were delusional, perhaps the effects of a chemical imbalance or temporary mental illness caused by the trauma of grief. Regardless of why or how those things happened, the results are not delusional. The results are real and solid.

Now, many years later, it seems clear to me that the helpless, the children, the orphans, are the very heart of God, and this mission was waiting for me to respond.

I don't know exactly how or why my son Fred died. I know he died at home, lying on the patio of his apartment, his fists clenched, and his body in convulsions from the extremely high temperature that he suffered. I know that, because a neighbor saw him—saw him in convulsions, saw his legs twitching in the final stages of death before calling the LA sheriff's department. I know that it took them more than 45 minutes to respond, and I know that his body core temperature was 105° four hours after his death. I also know that the vision of him lying there alone in death will never leave my memory.

If it had not been for all the difficult experiences in my life, all the mistakes and challenges, there might not have been the opportunity to rescue and change the lives of hundreds, perhaps thousands of children. If it had not been for the difficult experiences, I might not know the joy and wonder of seeing each of these beautiful children's smiles as they grow and learn and build their lives and shed the mantle of shame that they have had to drag along with them.

A visitor to Casa Hogar Los Angelitos, while looking at the dedication plaque in the center of the memorial garden, wiped tears from his eyes and he said to me "Nancy, I feel that I need to give you the message that the Holy Spirit has given to me. Your son Freddy had to live and die so that this work could happen."

My eyes filled with tears at the thought, at the loss, at the memory. I miss my son so much, but this message gave me a sense of peace as I contemplated that my son had to live and die so that children could be rescued.

What I have accepted as truth regarding my son's death is that I have been tremendously blessed with the opportunity to turn my inside sadness and grief outside of myself and into something that I could never have dreamed of: rescuing children and changing lives.

What I have learned about God is that the angels of the children always have an audience with Him, that He doesn't promise that we will not have tragedies, disappointments, and tears, but He embraces us in our tears in the midst of our tragedies, life circumstances, and heartache. I have learned that He knows my heart and that regardless of where I am in my life, He is always there leading, guiding, helping, waiting.

It is said that adversity makes opportunity, and I have certainly been given a lot of opportunities. I hope you don't have to go through all the mistakes, disappointments, and grief that I have gone through. It might not take a tragedy to open your hearts to the vision and mission that God has planned for you. I pray that your brokenness and pain can be seen as a challenge for healing by seeing yourself through spiritual eyes and choosing to do and be what God has called you to be—to answer whatever and wherever your calling might be with love, gentleness, joy, and faith.

To be willing to pursue that goal in the face of obstacles, difficulties, and discouragement, to decide in your heart not to give up, regardless of the setbacks and obstacles—to always remember that we may have events in our lives that momentarily defeat us, but that is different from being a "failure." It is the power of persistence that helps us to shake it off and climb back out of the hole.

We each have only a certain number of days in our lives. Each day is a portion of that life.

Most important is that we make each day count, wherever we are and however we can. Some of us are called to care for or rescue children. Others of us are called to show kindness to others—to offer a helping hand to care for the elderly, to bring food and clothing to those without, whether it might be next door or across the ocean.

Jesus said, "Many are called but few are chosen." I never really understood that, nor do I pretend to understand now.

But when I asked, "Then who *is* chosen? How and why would some be chosen and some not?", a young pastor friend said to me, after giving it some thought, "Those who answer the call are the ones who are chosen." I like that answer; it seems to make a lot of sense.

There was a story I heard about the famous Monastery off the coast of France—Mont St. Michel. One of the monks responsible for giving tours was talking about the history of St. Michel, and how, at the end of time, we would all face our judgment day. This statement was questioned by one of the visitors.

"I thought we had to face our judgment upon death. Well, how could that be?" he said. "Our lives continue to gather both good and bad through those we have influenced and those they influence and so on, until the end of the world. Each act of kindness, each life that is changed, each affect or ripple from our lives is accumulated and continues until the end of time, and only then can there be a final judgment of our lives."

That definitely put things in a different perspective for me. Each person of my past, each person who has touched my life, has contributed to whatever my life has become. I am grateful for them and hope that my life will touch others, and each life that is changed will ripple and continue to build for good.

So don't get tired of doing what is good. Don't get discouraged and give up, for we will reap a harvest of blessing at the appropriate time.
Galatians 6:9 (New Living Translation)

And to my son, Freddy—because you shared your life with us, because God heard your mother's prayers, His love will flow out to all of these children, giving them *faith*, *hope*, and *peace* and changing their lives forever. Thank you for letting me show my continual and undying love for you this way. Freddy, I love you.

And, thank You, God, for being the Father who loved me so much that you caressed my soul during the lonely times, carried me through the hard times, and held me during the sad times. You blessed my heartaches so that they could become wisdom, my tribulations so that I could learn patience, and my life so that I could touch the lives of children.

> Blessed is she that believed: for the Lord will perform those things which were told her...
>
> Luke 1:45

> How blessed is he who considers the helpless.
>
> Psalms 41:1

I am most blessed.

Nancy

APPENDIX

Poverty and ignorance is a breeding ground for crime, prostitu-tion, and drugs. Breaking the cycle of poverty is a bridge that can help defeat the power that crime and illegal activity has over those trapped in the hopelessness and desperation that poverty fosters.

The Children's Foundation, Loveland, Colorado, works in Mexico to rescue children in desperate situations through Casa Hogar Los Angelitos.

Thousands of children have been cared for and nourished, and others have been rescued and brought into full-time permanent care, changing their lives forever. Restoring opportunity for future self-sufficiency to children from birth through adulthood.

WHY MEXICO?

There are millions of children in Mexico who desperately need help. Our mission is to find a way to reach out to these children, to rescue more and more every day. Our responsibility is to stay focused on the mission and not get side tracked by the distractions of politics, criticisms or other obstacles and stones thrown in our path.

There are millions of children suffering all over the world, including in our own prosperous nation, the United States of America. However, Mexico is where I have been called. It is not the popular, trendy, or exotic destination that many seek, but it is in tremendous need, and it is where my heart reaches out.

Working in Mexico has proved to be difficult from many angles.

As a foreigner, I have to be careful and aware of everything I do and say. Financially, it is very difficult to find U.S. citizens, organizations, or businesses that see the need or want to help with projects in Mexico, and it's almost impossible to get Mexican citizens to trust enough to help. Large U.S. or world philanthropic organizations aren't drawn to the work in Mexico because of the known potential for corruption and legal hassles.

I was told by a large non-profit organization that Mexico is one of the top three most difficult and expensive countries for them to work

in, so they put their efforts elsewhere. Another organization told me
Mexico just doesn't give as much "bang for the buck" to their contrib-
utors because of the high cost of living and construction in Mexico
compared to other countries.

As a nation, Mexico is very proud and although strides have been
made in general, Mexico has been reluctant to admit to, or expose,
the seriousness of the poverty and child abuse within their borders
to the outside world.

Many times it seems that people who give to alleviate devastation
in other parts of the world do not seem to consider helping their own
next-door neighbor, Mexico, even though her children suffer from the
same devastation, crime, and poverty as these other children.

From a political perspective, there seems to be a battle going on
that affects people's attitudes toward helping anyone in Mexico, and
in the juggling or spinning of information and politics and media influence, many times the real underlying issues are ignored.

More than 60% of Mexico lives in some level of poverty, 20–30%
in extreme poverty—not poverty based on the same dollar amount
as we have here in the U.S., or with sufficient social programs to help
relieve that poverty, but poverty based on such a minimal or zero income that it is impossible to ever afford to eat more than tortillas,
chilies, and sometimes beans, to live in a stick shack, under a plastic
tent, or with the pigs in a corral. Yet we seem to see the poverty in
Mexico in a different light.

Poverty in Mexico seems to look better than poverty in other third
world or developing countries. Perhaps the psychological view we
have of poverty in Mexico as tourists and travelers is rainbow colored
because Mexico has trees and beautiful beaches. Everything looks
better under a tree or on a beach, especially if you are a tourist, staying in a comfortable hotel.

More than 300,000 children under the age of 15 are in forced labor
without any possibility of education or hope for the future other than
the life they have. Statistics in Mexico for 2006 show that the average
grade completion in school was only 6.7. Mexico is one of the worst
three nations (along with Cambodia and Thailand) for foreign sexual

exploitation of children, with most of that exploitation the result of visitors from the U.S. and Canada.

Our concern in the U.S. is for people spilling over our borders illegally, but people with hope, opportunity and food to feed their families don't need to cross any borders illegally, nor do they want to leave home, family and familiarity if they have any other option.

While we should make sure that our borders are protected from all unwanted and illegal aliens, perhaps we should begin to think about how we can find long term solutions at the root of the problem, which is, I believe, helping to provide education, hope and opportunity for our next door neighbor, so that the next generation of Mexicans can develop in a healthy way and be successfully productive in their own country.

I was on an airplane a few years ago, talking with the person next to me, and he gave an interesting illustration in reference to helping Mexico. "If you are a person with means, having a lovely home, car, fruit trees in your yard and all the other necessities, much more than you need or even use, and next door to you is a family that has fallen on hard times, they've lost everything except the land they live on. Their yard is bare, they have no car, house to live in or other basic necessities, what would you do?

"Would you build a high fence out of fear that these neighbors might sneak into your yard at night and take some of the fruit from your trees, close all your windows and doors, and make sure that you didn't pass by their property on your way to the store, so that you were not affected by their plight, would you consider going through your closet and pulling out some of your extra clothing, going out into your yard and picking fruit from your own trees, putting these things and other extras in a container and taking them over to your neighbors? Would you consider asking a group of people to go together and help this family, collecting funds and helping provide what they might need to help them leave this situation? What would you do?" this man asked.

Mexico and the children of Mexico are our closest neighbors in location and history, culture, as a trade partner, providing labor for our own projects and, of course, has provided some of our most popular culinary enjoyments. It is something to ponder.

> Suppose you see a brother or sister who needs food or clothing, and you say, 'Well, good-bye and God bless you; stay warm and eat well,' but you don't give that person any food or clothing, what good does that do?'
> James 2:15 (New Living Translation)

Today, obviously, there are other issues involved that have to be addressed, not the least being the brutality of the drug cartels and drug traffic throughout Mexico, pushing across the borders of the United States, creating a dangerous and volatile situation within Mexico and the border towns on both sides.

With illegal immigration and Mexican drug violence dominating the news about Mexico, there's another, hidden crisis that few people know about or consider. It is the hundreds of thousands of Mexican families living in extreme poverty. With makeshift shelters taking the place of homes, families are broken up as parents move frequently in search of low-paying jobs, and children are at constant risk of the ravages of human trafficking, sexual exploitation, and the drug trade. It is easy to become overwhelmed by the magnitude of the problem.

CASA HOGAR LOS ANGELITOS

Nancy with children at the casa hogar

In spite of this dismal situation, there is hope, and there are solutions. In the U.S., we have an opportunity to support this critical humanitarian need. Not only can we forever change the lives of children who face a desperate future, we can help build a new generation of self-sustaining people, thereby lessening future dependence on the resources of other nations.

I believe that every child is a precious gift. Experiences and perceptions affect a child for his lifetime, and learned responses will repeat over and over again. It is during childhood that our core values and beliefs are developed. It is the framing of the child that provides the finished adult. Investing in healthy, educated, and well balanced children is the most important investment that we can make for the future of the world.

Hundreds of children have been cared for as they have come through Casa Hogar Los Angelitos. Each child has their own story, a story about where they came from and the pain that they suffered through Most are heart-wrenching. I have only shared a few stories because of the need to protect the children. We cannot change the past or the horror that many of these children have seen; however, we can change the present and we can help them to change the future.

Through Casa Hogar Los Angelitos, we do more than just take impoverished children off the "streets" or provide food for various days—we provide nurturing and individualized resources and education that enable them to do more than merely survive, and we enable them to thrive and to become self-sufficient adults. By taking a hands-on approach to meeting the unique needs of each child, we can ensure the needs of each child are met and that he or she has the best possible opportunity for a positive, self-sufficient future. Going beyond our primary services, we provide cultural programs that enable the youth we serve to develop a greater understanding of their history and cultural pride that further solidifies their healthy esteem and the ability to make positive life choices.

Recognizing and understanding the deeply rooted cultural and political differences between Mexico and other countries enable us to prevent the loss of resources to crime or corruption and provide essential services that integrate effectively with the communities in which we operate.

THE PELAYOS

Many times we have the opportunity to eat at El Indio, a beach restaurant owned by the Pelayo family. From the beginning, this family has shared in the vision to help the poor children of Manzanillo.

When we have volunteer groups come down from the states or Canada, we have been able to make arrangements with the Pelayo family to stay open after their normal afternoon hours and provide dinner for our groups. It is always a treat because the food is excellent, the ambiance with the palapa roof and open air is wonderful, and we can walk the beach to get there and return the same way.

However, this night was special, because we had the good fortune to be able to share some of the miracle stories that have happened since we began this work, and some of the very people—members of the Pelayo family—who were part of the story or witnesses to the story were there sharing their version and their hearts as well.

FELIPE

My name is G. Felipe Pelayo Robles, and I come from a very large family in Manzanillo, Mexico. My father, Indalecio Pelayo, passed away at the age of eighty-three in October 2010 after a very full and good life. My mother, Cristina Robles de Pelayo, together with my father, had twelve children.

I was fifteen years old when I first knew the Nystrom family. I was one of the best surfers de la época. Robert Nystrom, David and Nancy Nystrom's youngest son, was only eight years old when Sr. David took him to an area called "olas altas en Santiago" where your "servidor" first met him. I went to the playa [beach] and was surfing every day to practice my favorite sport.

One day, I was riding my four-wheeler to the "boquita de Miramar" and my nephew, Ricardo Pelayo (son of my relative Aurelio Pelayo, an old friend of the Nystrom family), was with Robert. Robert seemed very bored to me, and he asked me if I would give him a ride back down the beach to his house, Casa Serena. I only lived about a block from there in a little apartment at the restaurant that my parents owned. Robert invited me in, and I told him that in the morning I was going to go surfing and would he like to go.

Lupita Carbajal, Felipe Pelayo, and Dr. Guiber Nuñez with Nancy

That was in January 1985, and from that time we became close friends. The Nystrom family has been an inspiration for me, and God has used this beautiful family not only as a blessing for my family, but also as a blessing to everyone that knows them.

Pablo and Nana (Paul and Lucille), the mother of Sra. Nancy, who came many times with them to Mexico, were always gentle, compassionate, and loving to those in the community. Nana was like a gift from God for our family.

When I was twenty years old, Sra. Nancy invited me to Vail, Colorado, United States, for the first time, and I was able to get my visa on this occasion in Juarez, Chihuahua. It was a very pleasant time—everything was new for me. I learned to understand and write English much better. It was in the Nystrom home that I first met Jesus Christ face to face when I had a personal experience one night with my Lord Jesus. From there, my life will never be the same.

The following winter, I was invited by a very special friend, chef Juan Carlos Madrigal, to work in a restaurant one hour and forty-five minutes north of Manzanillo in a resort area called Careyes. Close to the end of the season, the Nystroms visited me there. They brought my younger sister Cristi and a proposal to help me to make a bar in the restaurant of my parents, and I accepted this blessing.

In 1994, one week after the death of Sra. Nancy's son, Fred, God transformed my life. The death of Fred was like a bucket of cold water poured on my life. He was a good friend when I traveled to California to vacation with Robert. Fred attended us so well, right after his painful appendix operation, taking us everywhere and especially to know the famous Chinatown in Los Angeles. We ate without shoes and felt like we were in the clouds, going to Malibu beach and Huntington Beach with Robert and I always looking for a chance to surf.

When Sra. Nancy returned to Mexico after the death of Fred, I was attending church at the Iglesia Cristiana Perdón y Amistad. Sra. Nancy was still suffering with the pain in her heart after the loss of Fred, my brother in soul, but she never let her sadness show in front of us—she always seemed happy.

One day Pastor Saúl decided to call a group together in the house of one of my brothers, and this night we prayed to God for the poor and abandoned children of our country. The next day I went very early to Casa Serena, the house of the Nystrom family on the beach. When I came for my coffee, Sra. Nancy was on the terraza upstairs outside of her bedroom. I thought she had seen something in the ocean because she was calling me to come upstairs quickly. "God has shown me a vision," she said, and she began to relate all the experiences and things that God had told her to do. I told her that we had been praying for God to help the children of México, and God had answered our prayers quickly!

Months after God had said to Nancy "Feed my children," she still didn't know how or where to begin. I think that God told her what to do but didn't give the whole packet, because if He had told her everything, it would have seemed impossible to fulfill the vision. However, in the case of Nancy, even under difficult circumstances, she remained firmly determined.

We began to look for a location in Salagua and in a very poor area. Sra. Nancy told me that she liked a small property we saw that was on a corner. I was amazed—the property belonged to my father! So we asked if he would lend the property to us to begin the work to prepare hot food and invite all the very poor families.

My work was to go out and collect the food from the markets— 5 de Mayo of Manzanillo and the Mercado Colimense of Santiago; also from restaurants, milk companies, tortilla factories, and anywhere I could to find food to use for this project and prepare hot meals for the poor children and families of the area. This way, we fed so many children every day for almost five years.

My work continues as I help with the youth of the casa hogar and continue to give my support where ever I can.

JOSÉ—MY LIFE BEFORE CASA HOGAR LOS ANGELITOS

Hello and God bless you. My name is José. I was born in Manzanillo, Colima, México, in the year 1985.

This is just part of my history from my childhood before I met my God-Send Mom and Dad Nystrom.

I want to make it clear that I forgave my parents years ago because I'm not one to judge. Both my parents came from abusive backgrounds. Although I do not blame them, unfortunately, they did not meet good people like I did in my life to better themselves.

I am very conscious about not wanting to repeat their cycle, and I try not to dwell on my past but live in the present.

My memory takes me back to when I was three years old. We just got back from Chihuahua, where my mom is from, and everything seemed normal. I remember cutting my birthday cake surrounded by many kids and neighbors. My Dad was working as a bartender at a hotel. That's when my dad started drinking heavily and coming home drunk and filled with anger and started hitting my mom.

Now I am about to turn 4 years old, and one morning before he went to work, he took the cord from the iron and was peeling off the plastic of the cable, and I asked him, "What are you doing?"

He answers, "This is a whip that I'm going to hit you with if you misbehave."

So the days went by, and on Christmas day, a kid from the neighborhood was trying to take my new battery toy car and bullying me, so he keeps pulling on my car. When he finally took it from my hands, he fell back and started crying. His Dad comes out drunk and angry telling my dad, who was also drunk, to reprimand me because the kid says I hit him. Then my dad brings out the copper whip and grabs me by my hair and starts whipping me all the way to the house. Once we were in the house, he takes me to the bedroom and locks the door and keeps beating me. I hear my mom in the background screaming *Let me in* and banging on the door. At that point, he finally gets tired, and my body is filled with cuts and blood. My mom walks in, and my dad walks out of the room. My mom starts to comfort me, then she sees the blood and cleans the cuts.

The next day my dad was filled with guilt and remorse, but that didn't last long, as the physical abuse continued. Then we went to Acapulco to see my dad's older brother, and my dad got a job on a ship where he met a new woman and started to have an affair with her. My mom found out and made a big scene on the ship, which led to him getting fired. We ended up going back to Manzanillo on November 1, 1990.

I was about to turn 5 years old, and my mom was pregnant with my sister Brianda. I remember my dad hit my mom for being pregnant and kicked her out of the house, because he thought it wasn't his baby. That was his excuse to be with that other woman. I heard my dad say he was leaving and that we "were going to starve to death, you dogs," and he left. And then they got divorced.

At that time my mom could barely support us, because my sister was another mouth to feed. So she took me and my brother to an orphanage in Colima for a few months. My dad found out from relatives that my mom took me to an orphanage. He came with my stepmother—the one he was having an affair with on the ship—and took me to Oaxaca to live with them for a year or two. My life with them was very hard because we had no running water or toilet. I also had to walk very far to the water well and bring water to the house. I re-member that the first time my step-mother hit me, she told my dad, "I hit your son today because he misbehaved."

I remember hearing my dad saying, "Yeah, hit him every time he misbehaves." I was 5 years old and just doing what 5 year olds do.

After my dad told her that, she used that authority to abuse me all the time. She would hit me with anything in her reach. One time she hit me with a metal spatula, and it made several cuts in my head and blisters on my skin from the hot oil on the metal spatula that she was cooking with. After the abuse from my dad and step-mom, I started to run away to the neighbor's house or the river, anywhere to get away from them. One of the times I ran away, I came across a house where there were a couple of older boys who offered me a glass of milk because I was thirsty. I drank it, but it turned out not to be milk but spackle mixed with water. It was one of the worst days of my life, because I got so sick that I couldn't even go to the bath-room for days.

Another time I ran away, I met a lady who had a kid my age, and she gave me a lot of mangoes to take home. I was so excited and proud to bring all these mangoes home. When I got to the house, my step-mom started accusing me of stealing the mangoes, so she took me back to the lady's house. The lady told my step-mom I didn't steal them: "I gave the mangoes to him." It made me feel very sad to be ac-cused of something I did not do. I never told my dad because I was very afraid he would beat me and get mad at me for no reason. At some point, he got tired of me running away and took me back to Manzanillo.

On the way there, my dad said, "If your mom left for Chihuahua, I'm just going to leave you there." So during the drive back I was very scared that my mom wouldn't be there and I would be all alone. She was there, and my dad left me with my mom, and we never heard from him again. I was 7 years old.

When I got back, my mom was pregnant with my little brother Javier with the man whose mother lived in our building. But he and my mom were going through a breakup. She was very depressed because she really was in love with him, but she found out that he was involved with someone else. He eventually got a job in San Francisco, California, and we never heard from him again, nor did he ever claim responsibility for his son that he had with my mother. After he left, my mom became very irresponsible, depressed, and careless. She would leave me and my brother and sister in the morning by ourselves with no food.

My Mom was selling Avon products for a very short time, and from the money she made, my older brother took a few coins without asking. My mom burned his hands on the stove. It was very horrifying to see my brother scream with pain—he was only 8 years old. And I thought I was going to be next. So at 7 years old, I started working —cleaning onions at the mercado or helping the neighbors take their trash out or go to the store for them. I'd get a few pesos to be able to eat. I learned that life was a difficult game to play and that only by working was I able to eat. I also felt it was my responsibility to take care of my younger brother and sister, because one time a lady gave my sister a chicken to throw in the garbage and instead my sister ate it. She got very sick from it, and she almost died—and it was because she was so hungry, as we had no food in the house. I felt I needed to do something to make a little money for my sister and brother, too.

One day, an angry mob came to my house and broke the front door lock, accusing me of stealing a bicycle. I had no idea what they were talking about, so they burst into my house and looked everywhere, even under my bed. Obviously there was no bike at my house because I never took it. But it made me realize that people could be judgmental and mean—instead of helping us, they accused me of being a thief because I was poor. I always felt like the target of humiliation because I didn't have a "normal" family and because we were poor. Some people like to kick you when you're down just to make the point that they're better than you. We are all human beings with the same rights, and we all have feelings too; yet I was never

treated that way when I was a child. This always made me feel different and that I was not accepted.

A year passed, and my older brother got a job helping a family at
the swap meet. Then he went to live with them, mainly because he
was molested by a neighbor. I was 8 years old and had never been to
school. I got a job as a "flame thrower" at night in the streets, and
sometimes I would swallow the diesel by accident, and it would
make me very sick. I felt like I was dying, and in reality, I *was* dying. I
cleaned windshields during the day at an intersection and there was
another kid working in that same intersection juggling balls. Tragi-
cally, he was hit by a truck and died. It scared me a lot being in that
intersection, but I had to work so we could eat.

If I hadn't met Nancy and David Nystrom and had instead stayed
in the streets, I would not be alive now. I was 10 years old. I felt
hopeless and sad without knowing what real love was until I met
Nancy and David Nystrom. I met Nancy when I was in the streets and
she was in her van. She had come out to say that she had this place
where we could go and eat for free. The next day I went there to eat
and then continued to go almost every day. Then one day she came
over and took pictures of where we were, and when she was leaving I
felt a big urge in my heart to ask her for help. So I went to the window
of her van and asked her for help, and she said she would. That same
day, we went to my house and took pictures of the inhumane conditions that I was living in. She took me to her house to get me off the
streets.

Later I met Nana, Pablo, Gavin, Mathew, Jackie, and many more
angels who made a big change in my life. If it wasn't for all these
beautiful angels in my life, I would not be around today to tell you my
story. I was the first kid to enter and have the privilege to be able to
go to Casa Hogar Los Angelitos and be rescued from the streets, I was
able to go to school and have food in my stomach, and felt very loved.
I am older now, and I know I became a much better person today

only because of Nancy and David who save children in every aspect
of their lives.

Thank you, God, with all my heart!

GUIBER

Our lives are not defined by our vocations...we make a living by what we
get, but we make a life by what we give...who we are inside and what our
lives mean to others.

My name is Guiber Nuñez Matildes. I am the first child of parents
who began their marriage and then separated. I really don't know the
reasons why they separated; my sister, Betsaida Nuñez, was in my
mother's womb when evidently things became bad between this
lovely couple.

My mother left to find work after my sister was born. I remember
the day my mother left to look for work in the capital of Guerrero,
Chilpancingo, and for me that began a long time without seeing my
mother. When she returned I asked her, "Did you bring money?"

She responded, "No, I didn't find any work."

I told her, "See, and it took you a long time." It was very difficult
for my mother, a woman with courage and devotion. After a time, she
was able to find work in a small clinic, as she is a great nurse. She left
our pueblo to establish herself in a community—Huamuxtitlan, Guerrero—which was very far away from us.

My sister and I were cared for by and lived with our maternal
grandparents, Don Nicolás Matildes Zúñiga and Doña Elizabeth Ramírez
García. They raised us and educated us. My grandfather was a man
who lived his life with integrity and honesty, and my grandmother
was strong and firm. They were farmers—campesiños—peasants,
but peasants with a great desire to know the Word of God. They
helped to establish a Presbyterian Christian Church together with my
uncle, Guadencio Ramírez Matildes in our town of Tecoanapa.

My uncle lived in the United States of America in a town called Yuba City. Every year, he came to Tecoanapa and brought candies, piñatas, and a lot of gifts for the children. We had a dining area in the church where every morning we were given breakfast before going to school. After returning from school, we had to go to the campo to work. Those of us who were children and students would take lunch to the peons (laborers) and then we would begin working and work until dark.

Some days we would play with the bats in the areas where the trees would grow close together and their leaves would make a dark tunnel. The bats would fly past our heads, and we would try to hit them with a stick because we were afraid of them. My childhood was spent by the side of my grandparents, going to school, working in the fields. It was a fun time and filled with learning experiences. My grandfather is a man who knows so much history and is a very cultured but self-educated man. The "vice" that he has now is reading. He is a ninety-six-year-old man who can read without glasses. I compare him with a *roble*, a solid and strong oak tree. He is my hero, a person who understands and knows many things, and I have learned many things from him.

Every day when we were eating in the fields, we would sit on a tree trunk or on a rock below a tree. My grandfather always had something to show me or teach me or would ask me what I learned in school that day. I always preferred to listen.

One day when I was eight or nine years old, I used a machete to open a can. The bottle top hit me in the right eye. I remember that when the bottle cap hit me I felt an intense pain. Later my eye was completely closed, and I was blind in that eye. With my left eye, I saw the concern on my grandfather's face. He told me that I needed to return to the house so that I could be attended by a doctor. I began walking back, thinking what was going to happen to me. I put my hand over my good eye and tried to see with my right eye. But I couldn't. I sat on one of the rocks that was on the path and looked up at the blue sky, with a few distant clouds. I saw the green fields, the hills in the distance that were greenish blue, and after taking a little time, I started to pray to God. I began, "God, I would like to be a great preacher, but I can't become a great preacher with only one eye. What could I tell the people—that God has a damaged preacher? I know that for sacrifices you require a lamb that is unblemished without sin or defect, and I don't want to have this defect."

My prayer was brief, but I had a tremendous desire for God to hear me.

I went on to my house where my mother, my grandmother, and my Aunt Mercedes looked at my eye and took me to the local doctor. He told us that I had blood inside my eye, that I had broken something, and then he put a patch on my eye.

Later in the evening my grandfather came home and prayed for me. Two days passed and that night I was thinking about a passage in the Bible that I had heard that said, "If you have faith the size of a grain of mustard seed, you can say to the mountain, move—and it will move." That is how I understood it. That's what I intended to do. This night I prayed for a mountain to be moved and that my eye would be healed. The next day when I woke up the first thing I did was open the window to see the hill that was not there, but the hill was still there, it hadn't moved.

So, the second thing I had prayed for was for my eye to be healed. Remembering what had happened, I began to take off the gauze to open my eye, and a miracle had happened. My eye could see only a little—but I could see! I began to replace the gauze again and stayed lying down a little longer, then got up and had breakfast. I decided not to tell anyone what was happening in my life in this time, and I knew that God was not going to fail me and was going to make me perfect again. That He was answering my prayer. I remember one work that was in my mind this moment, and I made a commitment to God that if He would strengthen me, I would preach His Word.

I attended high school in my town, and when I turned seventeen years of age, I graduated and went to Acapulco where I began my career studies in medicine. I returned every weekend to my town and then returned to Acapulco on Sunday again to continue my studies. The reason I returned to my town each weekend was to work in the fields, and in this manner, help my grandparents who continued working hard every day.

When I finished my career in medicine I went for one year to the Port of Manzanillo for my internship, and it was here that I met my wife, Emilia Carbajal López, who was doing her social service work as a nurse at the civil hospital, the same hospital where I was also doing my internship. After finishing my internship in Manzanillo, I went back to my pueblo and began my social service in a small and very poor community in the state of Guerrero called El Refugio. This community was extremely poor—children without shoes, with parasites, and socially abandoned.

I finished my social service in March of 2009. During this time, one Monday, my family and I decided to spend a day at the beach. The family all went in a passenger pickup used as a cab in that area and headed to Playa Ventura. This beach is a tranquil beach, but we had to pass by a community by the name of La Union. A group of police officers began following after us in a truck, without any apparent reason. Two of my cousins who were sitting in the back of the truck cab were suddenly hit by bullets—Josué was hit in the left arm with an R15 bullet, typically used by the police forces, and Carlitos my other cousin, was shot in the arm as well, and I was shot twice, once in the abdomen and the other in the right flank, into the muscle. When I was hit, I immediately remembered the promise I had made to God to serve, and I had not fulfilled that promise. I was confident that these manmade bullets would not affect my life and that I would not die. I spent the next week in the hospital of Acapulco Guerrero in recuperation and also spent days in reflection and meditation, thinking of the greatness of God and the power that He has over life and death and how no one else has authority over anything, because it is He who has control of our lives.

I returned to Manzanillo to marry Emilia, but my heart always desired to help my people.

Another time in Guerrero, my wife Emilia and I worked in a health center in the community of Charco, municipality of Tecoanapa, Guerrero. I went every Sunday in a truck that provided transportation to the people of the community. I remember us riding to the health center with our heads full of dirt and our hair red from the dust, as well as our eyelashes, brows, and the rest of our body. The people from this humble community were accustomed to this form of transportation, but we were not. We found it difficult, especially at the beginning. On occasion, there was no transportation, so we would have to walk the five hours from our house to this poor community and then we would spend the entire week eating tortillas, chile, eggs, and coffee in the morning, the same in the afternoon, and the same at night. This routine became very tiring for my wife, so we made the decision to return to Manzanillo. My wife went immediately, and I went later because I had to complete my contract with the state health department of Guerrero.

The people of this humble community have such need, that it is difficult to leave them without help, they have so much poverty, are without education, they suffer from malnutrition, helpless and defenseless. I didn't want to leave, but I had a wife that was now pregnant that I needed to care for her. I left the community, but with the hope that one day I can return with toys, shoes, clothes, food and other articles for these gentle people.

ADDITIONAL ARTICLES
AND SOME FINAL THOUGHTS

It is easier to build strong children than to repair broken men.
Frederick Douglass

CORAZÓN LASTIMADO: THE THERAPEUTIC USE OF EXPRESSIVE ARTS WITH CHILDREN AT CASA HOGAR LOS ANGELITOS

by Don Phelps, Ph.D., L.C.S.W.

In broken English, a 13-year-old boy asked if he could draw me a picture. I sat with him as he sketched a superhero figure he had seen on TV. He was amazingly talented and drew with great detail and passion. When he was finished he smiled, gave the picture to me, and proudly said, "For you. Welcome!"

It was my first day volunteering at Casa Hogar Los Angelitos (CHLA) in Manzanillo, Mexico. The orphanage has more than 50 children and is registered as a Mexican civil association. During the spring of 2011, I was able to spend an extended period at CHLA as part of a university sabbatical. I asked to volunteer at CHLA because of their outstanding reputation for working with "difficult to place" children in Mexico. Most of the kids come from toxic environments that include domestic violence, homelessness, physical and sexual abuse, prostitution, sexual assault, neglect, and abandonment.

During my professional career as a social worker I have been privileged to visit many orphanages around the world. Most of them provide for the basic survival needs of children, giving them minimal health care, clothing, food, and shelter. The kids survive but few thrive. They often repeat the patterns and lifestyles of the poor and abusive homes they grew up in. Because of the lack of resources, few orphanages effectively address the complex needs of traumatized children. CHLA came highly recommended as a place where I could observe a "success story" and learn how they do it.

I started my sabbatical experience at CHLA with the following questions: Why is CHLA so effective with "difficult to place" children, given their limited resources? Why are CHLA children more likely to remain in school and go to college? Why are their rates of teen pregnancies, drug use, gang involvement, and criminality so low?

I discovered many reasons for their success while I was there. They have dedicated staff, passionate volunteers, visionary leadership, and a holistic approach to child development. A surprising finding, and maybe the strongest reason for the success of CHLA, is the extensive use of expressive arts in the daily lives of the children there. The founder of CHLA, Nancy Nystrom, instinctively began using expressive arts at the orphanage when it started over 15 years ago. Children receive instruction in music and have regular access to instruments. They can train and participate in a highly skilled and prestigious troupe of dancers that perform traditional Mexican dances in local, national, and international performances. The kids have access to donated art supplies and regularly draw and paint. Many of the children participate in creative writing, journaling and poetry. Expressive arts are integrated into each stage of the child's development. Through a variety of programs, CHLA facilitates emotional and creative expression, heals psychological wounds, and accelerates developmental growth through its use of the arts. I have never seen an orphanage embrace the arts as fervently.

Art is an important and universal facet of human expression and is as old as human civilization. "The use of art for healing and mastery is at least as old as the drawings on the walls of caves" (Aron-Rubin, 2005, p. 6). Expressive arts include dance, drawing, drama, creative writing, painting, poetry, music, sculpture, and photography.

Professions such as art therapy, music therapy, and movement therapy require graduate-level training and special professional certifications in the United States. The therapeutic use of expressive arts by non-credentialed professionals and paraprofessionals in orphanages is different in that it simply focuses on the inherent therapeutic value of children participating in creative endeavors. Both approaches encourage creative expression, but the context, facilitation, and purposes are very different. Most orphanages would welcome the opportunity to have expressive art therapists but the lack of funding and the availability of these specialized professionals in developing countries usually limit their use. Instead, orphanages such as CHLA use expressive arts as a way to supplement the care that children receive. Most of these activities are facilitated by volunteers, clinical staff, or child care workers.

Creative arts allow children the opportunity for self-awareness and growth through self-expression. This has been shown to reduce stress and accelerate psychological and physical healing. For many children and adults imprisoned in German concentration camps in World War II, drawings and paintings were used to cope with the horrors they saw each day. Prisoners had to carefully hide their work as many were killed when their art was found (Orstein, 2006). They traded food for painting supplies, and used garbage, old boxes and newspapers to paint on. Paint was made from coal soaked in water, watered down rust and vegetable dyes. "They responded to an imperative psychological demand to put on paper what they saw and what they felt" (pp. 395-396). Painting and poetry were a way for them to survive and cope.

I began to use expressive arts as a young counselor in the 1980s out of pure desperation. I worked with adolescents who struggled with mental health and substance abuse problems. Traditional "talk therapies" did not seem to work very well. I started reflecting on my own adolescence and the activities that helped me cope with stress and family problems. Activities such as music, sports, poetry and outdoor adventure provided an outlet to express myself and help me manage stress and adolescent angst. Much to the dismay of many of my coworkers, who tightly subscribed to traditional approaches, I started incorporating expressive arts into my counseling sessions. As my successful outcomes with adolescents grew, so did the agency's support of my methods. I was allowed to hire licensed and certified art therapists, music therapists, dance therapists, outdoor adventure therapists and exercise physiologists in our residential treatment programs. These programs supplemented traditional individual, group, and family interventions. The organization found that successful treatment outcomes were higher for adolescents that participated in expressive therapies than those who did not.

Most of the children at CHLA have histories of trauma and several display symptoms of post-traumatic stress disorder (PTSD). For some, attachment bonds with primary caregivers were absent, disrupted or severed at an early age. This destroyed the trust and security essential for healthy emotional growth and relational intimacy. Early relationships provide the emotional, neurological and social foundations for our ability to love (Perry, 2009). During my stay at CHLA, I heard heartbreaking stories of domestic violence, physical torture, sexual abuse and assault, drug addiction, prostitution, extreme neglect, and abandonment. Past traumatic events are difficult for children to talk about. They have not yet learned the words to describe the internal sensations, memories, images, and snapshots. Painful emotions and horrific experiences are frequently repressed by the children as a basic survival mechanism (van der Kolk, 2002). Children with histories of trauma experience multiple losses and carry the toxic memories from their past. They have a higher risk of experiencing mental health problems as adults. The dissociative behavior and post-traumatic stress experienced as a result of abuse and neglect negatively impacts a child's ability live a healthy, satisfying life. Alice Miller (1984) wrote

> The truth about our childhood is stored up in our body and although we can repress it, we can never alter it. Our intellect can be deceived, our feelings manipulated, our perceptions confused, and our body tricked with medication. But someday the body will present its bill, for it is as incorruptible as a child who, still whole in spirit, will accept no compromises or excuses, and it will not stop tormenting us until we stop evading the truth. (p. 315)

Expressive arts have long been used with children to promote psychological health and social support. They offer children "a way to express their feelings, perceptions, thoughts, and memories in ways that words cannot" (Malchiodi, 2005, p. 9). Studies indicate that expressive arts assist in healing from childhood trauma and aid in overall mental health "by providing opportunities to share experiences in an empathic environment through symbolically expressing emotions in a concrete way" (Smilen, 2009, p. 381). The staff and volunteers at CHLA engaged and positively reinforced children in the creative process by providing a safe space for them to express themselves. Because most children enjoy drawing, painting, singing, and dancing, art is a simple way for children to learn multiple forms of expressions. Children are allowed to express themselves without judgment or criticism. They are given the ability to choose from a variety of creative activities which increases their sense of internal control and willingness to participate.

Supportive peers can also be of great asset in the creative process. Many expressive art activities at CHLA are done in small groups. This cultivates social interaction, mutual support, peer modeling and empathy development (Cumming & Visser, 2009). Completing a work of art or finishing a performance in the presence of supportive peers and adults can raise a child's confidence and self-worth. By creating and sharing in a safe and supportive group, children are able to break their sense of isolation and shame. They discover symbols, labels, and other forms of expression that accurately reflect their own inner landscapes. Bhagwan (2009) wrote "individuals do not exist as isolated, discrete or separate entities, but as interconnected beings whose growth, well-being and transformation are shaped by dynamic and fluid relationships between friends, family, the global community and a Higher Spirit within the Universe" (p. 226). I frequently observed older children teaching younger children how to dance, how to play the guitar and how to paint. I would hear comments from kids sharing drawings and poetry with their peers such as "This one looks really sad" or "This one sounds angry." They would ask each other questions about their art, give encouragement and comfort one other if the process brought up past issues or difficult emotions. Adult facilitators carefully monitored this process and also offered affirmation and validation.

Expressive arts assist in the healing process by altering a child's physiology. When children engage in expressive arts it alerts the parasympathetic system in their brain (Lane, 2005). Their breathing slows down, their blood pressure lowers and the body becomes more relaxed. This helps to reduce the physiological hyper-arousal, or "fight or flight" response, associated with stress. Creative expression modifies our biochemistry and improves our physical well-being. When children participate in the arts it actually changes their bodies.

The creative process causes specific areas of the brain to release endorphins and other neurotransmitters that affect brain cells and the cells of the immune system, relieving pain and triggering the immune system to function more efficiently. Endorphins are like opiates, creating an experience of expansion, connection, and relaxation. In conjunction with these physiologic changes, art can regularly change people's attitudes, emotional states, and perception of pain. (p. 122)

> Neurophysiologists have shown that "art, meditation, and healing all come from the same source in the body; they are all associated with similar brainwave patterns and mind–body changes" (p. 123). A child's age and stage of development "has a profound impact on how an educational, care-giving, or therapeutic experience will influence the brain" (Perry, 2009, p. 243). Children who are traumatized when they are very young will respond and cope differently than children who are traumatized as adolescents.

Because of the way the brain develops, from the bottom up and from the inside out, different areas of the brain are impacted during trauma depending on the age of the child. The younger a child is during the trauma, the more necessary it is to stimulate specific neuro- pathways that promote healthy brain development (Perry, 2009). Certain neuro-pathways in the brain are developed and others underdeveloped depending in the experiences of the child.

This is a significant problem in the conventional mental health approach to maltreated children; many of their problems are related to disorganized or poorly regulated networks (e.g., the monoamines) originating lower in the brain. Yet, our clinical interventions often provide experiences that primarily target the innervated cortical or limbic (i.e., cognitive and relational interactions) regions in the brain and not the innervating source of the dysregulation (lower stress-response networks). Even when targeting the appropriate systems in the brain, we rarely provide the repetitions necessary to modify organized neural networks; 1 hour of therapy a week is insufficient to alter the accumulated impact of years of chaos, threat, loss, and humiliation. Inadequate "targeting" of our therapeutic activities to brain areas that are not the source of the symptoms and insufficient "repetitions" combine to make conventional mental health services for maltreated children ineffective. (p. 244)

> Experiences of trauma are often kept in one's memory as sensations, symbols and mental images which can be difficult to access in traditional "talk" therapy or informal conversation. These memories are situated in the primitive sections of the brain and may not be part of their conscious awareness. Expressive arts help children manage experiences that are too difficult or painful to assimilate. In his research on child trauma, Perry (2009) found that activities such as dance, massage, music, yoga, drumming and other similar interventions provide the patterned and repetitive neural input to alter the lower stress-response networks of the brain and help children better cope with the symptoms related to their trauma. This could explain one the many benefits children at CHLA receive from participating in the dance troupe. They practice their traditional Mexican dances many times per week. Their performance shoes have taps on them that make a percussive sound when they dance. While they rehearsed, I often closed my eyes and listened to the rhythms being created. The children emphasized specific beats and memorized the dance by the rhythmic sounds being created.

A child's spiritual awareness and development can be improved by the use of expressive arts. In 2004, Broadbent found that the use of dance deepens "children's spiritual awareness and provides a context for the development of a kinesthetic intelligence, which allows children to embody and give expression to abstract concepts and ideas" (as cited in Bhagwan, 2009, p. 229). A study by Mountain (2007) reported that creative arts "engage children in learning that is intimately related to spiritual development, involving self-understanding, understanding relationships, wider environmental connectedness, and connection with the divine" (as cited in Coholic, Lougheed & Lebreton, 2009, p. 31). The arts engage the senses in a way that transcends the ordinary and mundane aspects of life. As children connect to their poems, songs, dances or paintings, they become more aware of their thoughts, emotions and core beliefs. This assists in self-discovery and self-understanding and helps them find meaning. The children at CHLA use the creative process to communicate their joy and pain to God. One teen told me "I feel God's strength and beauty in me when I dance." For her, dancing was a way to move beyond her heartache and connect with her strengths and competencies. I attended several worship services held at CHLA each Sunday. These are completely voluntary and I was amazed how many children willingly attended. I observed them singing, dancing and using their creative artist talents to connect with God.

During my sabbatical I observed children at CHLA make great strides in their development and healing by participating in expressive arts. They beamed with pride and confidence after a dance or musical performance. Paintings and drawings were used to communicate a wide range of emotions and experiences. It was as if the arts were a normal and regular means of expression for the children there. The use of the creative process in each child's life was planned, organized and well facilitated. The results were impressive and inspiring. Their dedicated staff and volunteers have been able to reach and engage hundreds of maltreated children through the natural restoration and rejuvenation that occurs when we dance, sing, paint, write and draw. While generalizations from a single case are certainly limited, the intention of this paper is to qualitatively add to the ongoing inquiry into the therapeutic use of art in orphanages throughout the world. Given the limited access to psychological resources in such settings, child care workers must be strategic in their methods and strategies. Expressive arts are a relatively inexpensive and an effective method to engage child who have experienced trauma. It is surprising that more orphanages have not incorporated them into their program.

Casa Hogar Los Angelitos uses expressive arts in a way that is fun, therapeutic and inspirational. Creativity and imagination serve as a catalyst in the children's emotional, social, physical and spiritual growth. Further trainings must be provided for child care staff and volunteers on ways to use expressive arts without practicing beyond their level of competence. Experts in art therapy, music therapy and movement therapy could create inexpensive and safe activities to use with some guidance on how to facilitate the process. Further research is needed in the use of the arts in orphanages throughout the world as there are many variables involved in determining what makes an orphanage successful in working with "difficult to place" children. If these talented kids are to thrive and blossom to their full potential, we must be open to all innovative, inexpensive and evidenced-based approaches that help kids heal from trauma.

REFERENCES

Aron-Rubin, J. (2005). *Child art therapy.* Hoboken, New Jersey: Wiley & Sons, Inc.

Bhagwan, R. (2009). Creating sacred experiences for children as pathways to healing, growth and transformation. *International Journal of Children's Spirituality*, 14(3), 225-234. doi:10.1080/13644360903086497

Coholic, D., Lougheed, S., & Lebreton, J. (2009). The helpfulness of holistic arts-based group work with children living in foster care. *Social Work with Groups: A Journal of Community and Clinical Practice*, 32(1-2), 29-46. doi:10.1080/01609510802290966

Cumming, S., & Visser, J. (2009). *Using art with vulnerable children.* Support for Learning, 24(4), 151-158. doi:10.1111/j.1467-9604.2009.01418.x

Lane, M. (2005). *Creativity and spirituality in nursing: implementing art in healing.* Holistic Nursing Practice, 19(3), 122-125. Retrieved from EBSCOhost.

Malchiodi, C. (2005). *Using art activities to support trauma recovery in children.* Trauma & Loss: Research & Interventions, 5(1), 8-11. Retrieved from EBSCOhost.

Miller, A. (1984). *Thou shalt not be aware: Society's betrayal of the child.* New York: Farrar, Straus and Giroux Publishing.

Mountain, V. (2007). Educational contexts for the development of children's spirituality: exploring the use of imagination. *International Journal of Children's Spirituality,* 12(2), 191-205. doi:10.1080/13644360701467535.

Ornstein, A. (2006). *Artistic creativity and the healing process.* Psychoanalytic Inquiry, 26(3), 386-406. Retrieved from EBSCOhost.

Perry, B. (2009). *Examining child maltreatment through a neurodevelopmental lens: clinical applications of the neurosequential model of therapeutics.* Journal of Loss & Trauma, 14(4), 240-255. DOI: 10.1080/15325020903004350.

Smilan, C. (2009). *Building resiliency to childhood trauma through arts-based learning.* Childhood Education, 85(6), 380. Retrieved from EBSCOhost.

van der Kolk, B.A. (2002). *In terror's grip: healing the ravages of trauma.* Cerebrum, 4, 34-50. Retrieved from EBSCOhost.

Dr. Phelps received his Ph.D. in social work in 1997 from the University of Illinois. He also studied at the George Williams College School of Social Work at Aurora University where he completed his Master of Social Work degree in 1990, focusing on youth and family therapy. He is a doctoral-level licensed clinical social worker.

Dr. Phelps is currently an associate professor in the School of Social Work at Aurora University near Chicago. Over the last 25 years, he has worked as a youth and family therapist, clinical director, chief operating officer and chief executive officer. He completed a university sabbatical in Manzanillo, Mexico, during spring semester 2011.

Don Phelps
Ph.D., L.C.S.W.
Aurora University—School of Social Work
347 S. Gladstone Avenue
Aurora, Illinois 60506
USA

630.844.4238
dphelps@aurora.edu

A newspaper article was in the *International Herald Tribune* (25 May 1995):

MEXICO CITY'S STREET CHILDREN
By Tod Robberson
Washington Post Service

MEXICO CITY — The morning sun streaked across 12-year-old Eloy's emaciated face as he and his girlfriend, Margarita, greeted the new day from a discarded red velour armchair they had shared the previous night outside a Mexico City subway station.

Both yawned, squinted, then simultaneously pressed toxic, solvent-soaked tissues to their mouths, inhaling deeply.

The momentary boost from the fumes was enough for Margarita, 14, to pull herself to her feet. Then, complaining of a fever and wanting more sleep, she stumbled a few meters over to a manhole, stepping around a dead rat and descending into her "bedroom"—an old underground pipe that years ago had run thick with raw sewage.

The story of Eloy and Margarita reflects that of thousands of other homeless Mexican children.

The section of rusted iron sewer pipe where Margarita crawled off to sleep is also home for 45 of Mexico City's poorest poor. They range in age from 7 to 19, spending their days begging, washing car windows at intersections, and foraging for food.

At night, they escape the pain and loneliness of street life by gathering in their underground culvert. Someone collects the day's earnings and rushes off to a nearby hardware store to purchase whatever "drug" is available—chemical solvents, shoe cobbler's glue, or plumber's pipe dope.

For reasons no one cares to explain, Eloy is the group's keeper of the tissues, stuffing wads of solvent-soaked toilet paper into a plastic bottle and dispensing them to all takers.

"It makes me fly," said Guillermo, 19, as he accepted a tissue from Eloy. "I can forget everything and take a trip."

A 1992, United Nations survey estimated that there were 11,000 "street children" in the Mexican capital, either homeless or put on the streets by their parents to beg or work.

Now, "We think there are 30,000 to 40,000," said Mr. Capellin, whose organization operates eight shelters for children across Mexico City. He added that no nationwide estimates exist.

Another newspaper article in the *Diario de Mexico* (30 April 1997):

STREET CHILDREN IN TROUBLE
by Kristen Smith

Over 13,370 children work in the streets, said Mexico City's Secretary of Education, Health, and Social Development, Javier Vega Camargo. Of those, 87 percent live on the street and are exposed to violence, drugs, and AIDS through sexual promiscuity.

"We are looking at a time bomb that's going to go off in everyone's face in five or ten years," said the director of Casa Alianza de México, referring to AIDS.

José Manuel Capellín Corrada estimates that 95 percent of street children take drugs, mainly in the form of inhalants like paint thinner and airplane glue.

"Right now the Mexican government is waging a 1.5-billion-dollar drug war. I wish they'd just spend a little of that on the war against inhalants," he said.

Street children also face violence from police and labor exploitation, but most of them cannot file a complaint with the México City Human Rights Commission because they have no birth certificates, said Vega. "Without a birth certificate it's as if they do not exist. They cannot file complaints. They can do nothing," he said.

The Education Secretariat's judicial branch registers around 90 children a day for birth certificates as part of its Alliance For Children, said Vegas.

"Mexico is in the process of education downsizing. In Mexico, there are more students than there are schools because of increased population and the (peso) crisis," said Gloria Ramírez Hernández. Public schools also lose approximately 41 percent of their students to attrition, she added.

An online article about the problem of neglected and abandoned children:

- UNICEF (United Nations International Children's Emergency Fund) has defined three types of street children: Street-Living, Street-Working, Street-Family.
  - *Street-Living Children*: children who ran away from their families and live alone on the streets.
  - *Street-Working Children*: children who spend most of their time on the streets, fending for themselves, but returning home on a regular basis.
  - *Street-Family Children*: children who live on the streets with their families.
- Mexico City has 1.9 million underprivileged and street children. 240,000 of these are abandoned children. (Action International Ministries)
- In 1996, the Inter-American Development Bank and UNICEF estimated there were 40 million children living or working on the streets of Latin America out of an estimated total population of 500 million. That equates to more than 12% of the total population being children living or working on the streets of Latin America.
- 8–11 million children under the age of 15 years are working in Mexico. (U.S. Dept. of Labor, "Sweat and Toil of Children," 1994, citing U.S. Dept of State, *Human Rights Report*, 1993).

Professor Martin Patt
"Street Children—Mexico"
(http://gvnet.com/streetchildren/Mexico.htm)

PEOPLE START TO NOTICE
THE CASA HOGAR LOS ANGELITOS

In 1995, newspapers were publishing editorials and trying to address the problem that continues to exist to this day. The *Mexico City News* ran a story entitled "Miracle In Manzanillo." This story talked about the problem of poverty and how it affects the children, and how, because of the vision of one woman, changes in Manzanillo were taking place through the vision to feed these children.

FOCO HISPANO
Vail Valley Times Al Servicio del Pueblo Latino   3 de Mayo de 1995

Milagro en Minturn (Key unlocks a mother's grief)

■ By Jessica Davidson
Times Staff Writer

Nancy Nystrom creía en milagros, pero también creía en trabajar duro en su galería de arte en Minturn, pasar tiempo con su marido y sus niños.

Cuando, inesperadamente su hijo de 28 años murió en septiembre, su corazón estaba destruido.

"No lo culpé a Dios," dijo ella, "Sentí que algo bueno sucedería como resultado de esta desgracia, que existía una razón por lo ocurrido que algún día sabría por que."

Dos semanas después del fallecimiento de su hijo, Nystrom y su marido visitaban el Colorado National Mounument cuando caminando sola ella escucho una vos que decia "alimenta a mis niños."

Nystrom no se considera a si misma una persona extremadamente religiosa, mismo asi, su fé siempre fue muy fuerte.

"No veo visiones" "no escucho voces" dijo ella, por lo menos hasta ahora.

De regreso en su hogar ella se encontraba atendiendo a un cliente en la Galería de Arte Windwood, cuando vio a una mujer que casi corriendo venía hacia ella diciendo: "Me manda el Espíritu Santo! alguien necesita mis oraciones."

Esta mujer colocó su mano sobre el corazón de Nystrom y le dijo: "Hay una llave en tu corazón, un llave victoriana, no se cual sea su proposito, pero esta allí."

Cuando esta mujer retornó al negocio unas semanas más tarde con una llave colgando de su cuello, una llave dorada, Nystrom pregunyto: "¿es esa mi llave?"

La historia de la llave

Un día, visitando Salt Lake City esta joven mujer se encontraba tomando un café con unos amigos cuando un hombre con aspecto de vagabundo se acercó a ella y le dijo: "Quiero decirle, señora, que dios sabe lo que usted esta haciendo," este hombre tenía colgada en su cuello un llave con un formato

Nancy Nystrom

muy especial. Sacándose la llave de su cuello se la dio a esta joven mujer diciendo que solo existían dos llaves como esta en todo el mundo y que sería de un gran significado para quien la llevara consigo. Una llave de dios que ella algun día daría a otra persona cuando la persona correcta apareciera.

"Ella supo en ese momento que ese vagabundo era un ángel, un mensajero de dios."

La llave es la llave

Nystrom conservó la llave en su cuello y contó la historia a su familia.

"Algo diferente esta sucediendo en mi vida esto no es algo normal."

La vida continuó sin grandes cambios hasta que un día, descancando en una calurosa tarde en Manzanillo México, ella recibió casi como un mensaje divino una claridad en los hechos y de inmediato supo que hacer.

Ella recordó aquella voz que le dijo: "alimenta a mis niños" y ella vió la necesidad de crear un orfanato en México.

Así fue que comenzó a hacer un dibujo de como sería el orfanato, con la sorpresa que al terminar el diseño gráfico, este tenía la misma forma de la llave mistriosa.

Pero ahora el problema era como conseguir el dinero para hacer este proyecto. La respuesta estaba en la llave.

Ella llevó la llave a un artista Mexicano amigo, Jesús, quien creó una replica de la llave como un trabajo de joyeria con una amatista en el centro de ella y 5 mil de estas llaves se vendieron al público como joyas obteniendo asi el dinero para la construcción del orfanato.

Nystrom comprendió que este no era su trabajo o su proyecto de negocios, este era el trabajo de dios a travez de ella por eso es que ella no se preocupa por que algo salga mal, dios va a proveer lo que sea necesario para que esto sea una realidad.

Semanas mas tarde todo comenzó a tomar forma : un misionario Americano se reunió con la iglesia para discutir la ayuda que se precisaría para este proyecto, otra familia mexicana se ofreció para ayudar en el mismo y otra gente ofreció su ayuda también, y todo comenzó a funcionar para lograr el milagro.

Nystrom dijo: "Dios me encomendó este trabajo y yo lo hare en honor a mi difunto hijo."

The News **LIVING**   Thursday, June 22, 1995   Mexico City, Vol. XLV No. 347   Thursday, June 22, 1995

A Miracle Is Taking Place In Manzanillo

By BLANCA ROBLEDA
The News Staff Reporter

When Nancy Nystrom's 28-year-old son Freddy Bckdahl died on Sept. 27, 1994, a series of what she considers to have been "revelations from God" took place.

These revelations brought about a single message in the mind of Nystrom: An orphanage must be built in Manzanillo in the state of Colima.

"I am a very spiritual person," says Nystrom, who lives in the United States and vacations at her home in Manzanillo. "I love God, but I am not a religious person. I have never seen visions. I am a conservative person and this is very unusual to me."

Since the revelation, although unbeknownst to Nystrom, several people have somehow heard about the story, and have approached her, attempting to help.

One of these people was Jose Luis Navarrete, the president of the Municipality in Manzanillo. "Building an orphanage in Manzanillo is very important because we receive many kids from different parts of the nation who do not have parents, and many become criminals or drug users," he said.

"Mrs. Nystrom's project represents a great opportunity for these children to rehabilitate themselves into society.

To this date, two portions of land have been donated for the orphanage.

"God made it clear, we were not to ask anyone for anything," she said. "He said, 'All you have to do is tell the story and I will touch the hearts of the people, and I will bring them, and I will provide everything that

is needed.'"

The largest parcel of land was given by the City Hall's Attention to Citizens Department. While arrangements are still being made, the land is located in the Francisco Villa *ejido* and could be as big as one to three hectares or more, depending on Nystrom's needs, as Navarrete explained.

A second piece of land was donated by private citizen Abel Salazar, who gave 1 hectare located some 8 kilometers from the town of Francisco Villa.

This is where the orphanage, to be called "Los Angelitos," will be built.

"Los Angelitos" is expected to lodge some 30 to 40 children or more, and will include offices and a clinic where a doctor can assist the children.

"But since there are two pieces of land," Nystrom says, "there should be two orphanages," Nystrom says. "As soon as we get the people, we hope to have another orphanage completed during a 5-year term. Together the two will lodge 200 children or more," Nystrom said.

After her son died, Nystrom prayed to God, asking for guidance and answers to her prayers.

Then God answered.

The first message came while Nystrom was walking in the Colorado Monument Park in the state of Colorado.

To her surprise and disbelief, the signal came as a soft voice saying "Feed my children."

The following day she heard the same message, and again the next day.

Nystrom was convinced. She began to read the Bible. She came a across a passage in

GUSTAVO BENITES
Nancy Nystrom and her inspirational key (below).

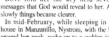

which Jesus was saying "If you love me, feed my lamb; If you love me, feed my sheep . . ."

"I knew that this was from God, but I still did not know what it meant," she said.

In the memory of her son, she and her husband had already set up a Memorial Scholarship Fund in Colorado, but there was something more to be done, she told herself.

Soon after, Nystrom was at an art gallery in Minturn, Colorado, where she met Jackie Trujillo or "Dove" as her friends call her. "Dove" said she was there because God had compelled her to do so. Destiny brought the women together. Each one knew the other needed support. On their second meeting,

Dove was wearing a bronze key on a necklace. Upon seeing it, Nystrom exclaimed, "That is my key."

Dove told her the key held several messages that God would reveal to her. And slowly things became clearer.

In mid-February, while sleeping in her house in Manzanillo, Nystrom, with the key around her neck, woke-up to a sudden idea: "We have to build an orphanage here."

Later, when Nystrom told a local fisherman, Felipe Pelayo, the details of her idea about the orphanage, and how she got them, Pelayo was surprised. He told her that his family and other locals had recently gathered with their pastor and prayed for God to help the children.

Today many people have offered their help from charity groups in Colorado to local architects in Manzanillo.

Says Nystrom, "The story has become a community story, a Mexico story, God's story."

People interested in contacting Nancy Nystrom should send letters addressed to her to The News, Balderas 87, 3rd floor, Col. Centro. 06040

LOCAL

From mother's pain comes Key of Hope

By Sara Kanouff
Daily Staff Writer

Sept. 27, 1994, was a day of excruciating pain, but it also was the beginning of a future filled with hope and significance for Nancy Nystrom, a Vail resident and owner of the Winwood Gallery in Minturn.

On that fateful day in 1994 her recently married, 28-year-old son, Fred Eckdahl, died unexpectedly. There was no warning, no time for goodbyes.

This crushed his mother; her pain was unbearable and ceaseless. In a desire to escape their grief briefly, Nystrom and her husband, David, took a trip to Colorado National Monument. While visiting, Nancy said, she heard a voice call to her softly; "Feed my children."

Stunned by the intensity and the message, she asked her husband if he had heard anything, but he had heard nothing. For the following two nights she heard the same voice with the same message at their campsite.

The couple returned to Vail and Nystrom fell into a deep depression. She could not shake the thought of her son and his unfair death. One night, while deeply confused and in excruciating pain, Nystrom drove aimlessly around town and ended up in a fast-food restaurant parking lot. She was sobbing uncontrollably and praying for some solace.

She asked God to hear her prayers and prayed for a sign He was listening. At that moment, in 4 degree weather, streams of rain were running down the windshield of her car. She looked to her right and saw ice on the car next to hers. She felt this was some kind of miracle and she was in the presence of the Lord. Nystrom writes:

"Then I realized, with a sense of peace and warmth that God had heard my prayer and had answered with what seemed to be tears of "angels"... on my windshield."

One day in December Nystrom was in her gallery in Minturn, weeping all morning. That afternoon a woman walked in and immediately approached Nystrom to ask her how she was doing. After Nystrom realized the woman actually felt her pain, she told her of the death of her son. The lady, called Dove, said to Nystrom, "The Holy Spirit sent me here today, do you mind if I pray for you?"

Nystrom was a bit frazzled, but freely accepted her help. Dove prayed for Nystrom. "A sense of peace and comfort engulfed me as she prayed. She spoke of things that God's spirit was speaking to me. I was amazed and humbled."

Dove explained to Nystrom that she could see a key in her heart and that this key would allow her to send a message of hope and peace.

Things returned to normal for Nystrom until Dove entered her gallery once again. Dove began to walk toward her and Nystrom said, "That's my key!" She said she did not know why she was requesting this key from around Dove's neck, but Dove agreed.

"Yes, this is your key."

Dove removed the key from her neck and handed it to Nystrom. Dove then told her the story of the key.

Significance of the Key

Dove explained that she was in Salt Lake City working and one afternoon decided to meet a friend for coffee. As she entered the coffee shop she noticed a scraggly man at the next table.

"The minute I saw this man I knew I was going to talk to him," Dove said. She invited him to join her table and she visited with them for a few minutes before he pulled out a map.

"He drew a circle in the center of the map on the location of my hometown and proceeded to tell me all the areas that I had been," Dove said. "He showed me the many states I had traveled and with his finger showed me that the path I had traveled was the shape of a cross."

She inquired how he knew where she had traveled and he said nothing, only smiled warmly. She then caught a glimpse of the key that was around his neck and told him that it was her key.

He acknowledged the piece and agreed it was, now, her key. He removed the key, handed it to Dove, and explained only two of these keys existed. He told her the significance of the key would become apparent to her in the future.

Dove then explained that she looked into the heart of the man and, saw it was made of gold. She felt this was an angel, a messenger of God.

Dove kept the key for two years and to her it coincided with *Revelations 3:7-8*... "These are the word of Him who is Holy and true, who holds the key of David. What He opens no one can shut, and what he shuts no one can open. I know your deeds, see, I have placed before you an open door that no one can shut. I know you have little strength, yet you have kept my word and have not denied my name."

The Key and its new significance

Nancy Nystrom, after accepting the key, was confused about the significance of the key in her life. One day she was discussing the key with her brother and the answer finally came to her.

"It's like the scripture *Jeremiah 33:3*, 'Call unto me, and I will show thee great and mighty things, which thou knowest not.'"

In February, Nystrom and her family went to their home in Manzanillo, Mexico. Nystrom was resting

Submitted to the Vail Daily
Nancy Nystrom designed the Key of Hope to benefit orphaned children. The project began last September and construction on the orphanage will begin this December in Manzanillo, Mexico.

in her home and was jolted with the thought, "There needs to be an orphanage for the children here."

"The thoughts were flooding through my mind and I felt compelled to begin writing everything down," said Nystrom. "I was writing as fast as I could, every detail was like a new inspiration."

She said it was then that she had the vision of the orphanage and its structure. She also said she was told that she was not to ask for anything, it would all come to her.

Next, Nystrom said, was another explanation of the key. She felt she should replicate it in silver and sell them to make the orphanage a reality. She brought the key to a silversmith in Taxco and he created the Key of Hope.

Vision to Reality

Nystrom received the vision, she said, but she did not know where she would get the land, architect or support for the endeavor.

Please see Key Page 5

Key

From Page 3

The promise in March allowed her to follow her dream, though, and travel to Mexico to wait for the answers to many of her questions.

When she arrived in Mexico she met with Gabriella Salazar, a friend who heard the story and wanted to help. Her father listened to the story one night along with 30 other residents of Manzanillo. Abel Salazar along with another group donated land for the project.

In three days Nystrom had the land she needed for the project, and she didn't ask anything of anyone, she said.

Nystrom still did not have an engineer for the project. That Saturday afternoon Sr. Birla and his son, Pedro Birla Miguel, entered her home, listened to the story, and the son offered his assistance in the project.

"It appears that God is raising an army of people and events to do his

work," said Nystrom.

Nystrom said that she hopes they will begin construction for the orphanage in December. The project is becoming a reality, but there are many ways that people can still help.

The Key of Hope is now on sale and will benefit the orphanage, which will be built in the shape of a key. The key is available at the Winwood Gallery in Minturn and La Plata in Crossroads.

"The events of the past months have not removed the grief and the pain in my heart, but God has brought comfort in purpose and in the wonder of his power and peace," said Nancy Nystrom. "My life is still being changed as this work has just begun. But whatever comes to me through the grief, the prayers, the 'revelations' of God's message and this very interesting key, I can start to smile and say, 'Look Freddy, what your life has brought and the love and hope that will flow out to children because you shared your life with us.'"

Feeding Mexican orphans: both body and soul

Children's Foundation changes lives for children in Manzanillo

PAM BOYD
Enterprise reporter

Orphaned children in Mexico lack the essentials of life — food, water, clothing and shelter. But most of all, they lack the resources to change their fates. Without education and nurturing, there's little chance these children can rise above the poverty and deprivation.

But for some of the orphans of Manzanillo, Mexico there is hope in the form of the Casa Hogar los Angelitos. This orphanage, opened in 2001, is a labor of love founded by former Eagle Valley resident Nancy Nystrom.

"These are lives that would be lost. We change these children's lives," she says.

Operated by a Colorado based non-profit corporation called The Children's Foundation, the orphanage is part of an overall effort that seeks to change the lives of children suffering from abuse, poverty, neglect, abandonment and to break the devastating cycle of poverty and abuse.

Opening an orphanage was never a dream of Nystrom's until tragedy hit her life on Sept. 27, 1994. On that day, her son Fred died unexpectedly. Nystrom was consumed with grief. At the time, she was living in Vail and was the owner of Winwood Gallery in Minturn. Through a series of events, she came to fervently believe that it was God's will for her to build an orphanage in the town of Manzanilla, where she and her husband had owned a home since 1983.

The Casa Hogar los Angelitos is home to 47 orphans. In addition to providing children with food and shelter, the facility provides tutoring so that the

Special to The Enterprise
Nancy Nystrom and one of the orphans from Casa Hogar los Angelitos in Manzanillo, Mexico.

orphans, who have seldom attended school, can keep up with their classmates.

"One of the things we teach our children is to give back," continues Nystrom. "Our children go out and help other people." Children from Casa Hogar provide outreach to Mexican migrant families — bringing clean water and food to families who labor long hours in the fields and live in makeshift tents made of plastic garbage bags. According to Nystrom, this outreach effort continues to grow and the orphanage has fed, literally, thousands of people.

Nystrom — "Mama Nancy" to the orphans — says the Children's Foundation is a nondenominational effort that is not associated with any single church, business, political group or government. "We are truly philanthropic in the fullest sense."

And she believes that one person can change the future by changing the life of a child. "They are all beautiful children. All they need is an opportunity," says Nystrom. She points to Rodrigo as an example.

Rodrigo was Casa Hogar's first resident. Before moving to the orphanage, he was surviving on the streets as a flame blower — he would spit flammable liquid from his mouth and light it on fire for the entertainment of passersby. "If he hadn't come to us, he would have died. His brain would have been fried or his lungs would have been fried," says Nystrom. "Rodrigo's goal now is to be the president of Mexico. I believe he can do it."

To learn more about Casa Hogar los Angelitos visit www.childrensfoundationinc.com

TWO STORIES

As I entered into the month of September 2004, I was reminded that it had been 10 years since God's anointing touched my heart and life, bringing the visions and calling that brought the works now called "The Children's Foundation," "Casa Hogar Los Angelitos," "Ministerios de Amor," and those other projects that the Holy Spirit has put into the hearts of others.

This was a special time of remembrance, and I was reminded of two Bible stories that had special meaning to me throughout these years, and perhaps they might have significance to others as well.

The first story is from Nehemiah and begins with Nehemiah in a foreign land going about his life as a lowly cup bearer for the King. God gave Nehemiah a burden and a vision to go and rebuild the wall that had surrounded the Holy City, Jerusalem, and was now destroyed and broken down.

Nehemiah left with volunteers to help him in his task; however, the people in the area resisted and resented the work that Nehemiah was trying to do.

There were no reasons given specifically, yet it became apparent that the main motives were jealousy, resentment, and false pride.

Even among those that had been chosen to help build the wall there were those who showed resentment of Nehemiah's leadership and authority and tried to undermine the work.

As the work continued, the people began to accuse Nehemiah falsely, causing rumor and dissension. They began to shoot arrows at the workers, threatening them, trying to stop the work. Even among his own work force, there was ridicule and undermining of Nehemiah's authority, ability, and intent.

However, as Nehemiah's determination proves—and as scriptures prove—the threat of attack, violence, ridicule, and undermining cannot stop those whose purpose is more important to them than even their lives. When false propaganda and fear take hold, those who are strong for God's purpose must regroup and redouble their efforts.

For the project to succeed, just as with any successful project, the people had to combine a right attitude with right action and work together supporting each other in order to accomplish the task.

Nehemiah continued amidst every kind of assault—personal, physical, moral, and spiritual. However, he worked to ignore the power of ridicule and peer pressure. He rejected their efforts of conspiracy, and to cause confusion with disruption, he carried a weapon in one hand and continued his work with the other hand. He developed a support system that would rally to the aid of those who were under attack, and he prayed, "O God, turn their reproach on their own heads."

The task was finished, and God did deal with those who had tried to undermine the work.

The second story that has been very important to me during several significant times—especially after laboring in prayer until 3 or 4 in the morning, wrestling with power struggles and the jockeying of position of others in this work—is the story of Gideon, found in the book of Judges, chapters 6–8.

In this story, God strengthens those He calls and commissions. Gideon had to trust in His abiding presence and to know that He would provide the resources of His wisdom and power through those He called and commissioned.

As the story begins, Israel is being oppressed and abused by the Midianites. There is none who has the authority or the apparent skill of leadership to fight against the oppressors or to free Israel from this enemy.

Gideon was singled out and called for this task, even though he was the least likely to handle the job, being the "least" of his father's house and belonging to a clan that was the weakest in his tribe. However, the Lord spoke to him and called him a mighty man of valor and said to him that he would defeat the Midianites even as one man. He became God's anointed for His purpose.

Gideon tested his own belief and acceptance of the calling, not once but twice, to confirm that he had in fact understood God's calling correctly.

So Gideon began to build a team, a force to go against the Midianites. But the Lord told him, "You have too many people." The Lord instructed Gideon to test the people and tell them, "Whoever is fearful and afraid, leave." A large number of men left, but the Lord told Gideon, "You still have too many people. If there are too many people, then they want to claim glory for themselves, saying, 'We have done this' rather than giving the glory to God."

So, the Lord told Gideon to give another test, and this time they were to go to the river and drink the water. The difference in their drinking styles decided whether they were alert and ready and prepared for the task. Now Gideon was left with only 300 men to fight the army of the Midianites who were "as numerous as locust" and heavily armed.

Then, as God had given instructions of how the battle would be fought, Gideon gave every man instructions to follow his lead, to wait and watch, and at the moment of command and not before, they would begin the battle, blowing the trumpets and breaking pots from the surrounding of the camp. They were to stand firm and follow exactly as they had been commanded and the Lord would deliver the army into their hands, which He did as the Midianites became confused and began to kill each other.

There are many lessons in this story, but the most important lessons for me have been to understand that many times the Lord chooses the most unlikely leader to accomplish His task, that He will give the strength and power needed when it is needed, and that He doesn't need a large army of people, just a small number of alert, dedicated, faithful people who will follow instructions without the interference of ego or self-important distractions when it's time to do the job.

And last—but perhaps not the least—is that we should be willing to accept and stand strong against adversity and opposition when it does come, and believe that God will use these trials to train us and strengthen us in spiritual understanding and determination.

I have learned also that I must test and confirm any sense of divine leading to be certain of God's direction and refuse to move impulsively or because of the pressure of others.

This poem was a favorite of my grandfather, Claude Barnes. I read it many times as I was growing up and always felt that it was something that my grandfather felt connected with. I, too, kept this in the back of my mind as a guide. If I could accomplish these goals, I, too, would be a person of real character—like my grandfather.

IF

If you can keep your head when all about you
Are losing theirs and blaming it on you;
If you can trust yourself when all men doubt you,
But make allowance for their doubting too;
If you can wait and not be tired by waiting,
Or being lied about, don't deal in lies,
Or being hated, don't give way to hating,
And yet don't look too good, nor talk too wise:
If you can dream—and not make dreams your master;
If you can think—and not make thoughts your aim;
If you can meet with Triumph and Disaster
And treat those two imposters just the same;
If you can bear to hear the truth you've spoken
Twisted by knaves to make a trap for fools,
Or watch the things you gave your life to, broken,
And stoop and build 'em up with worn-out tools;
If you can make one heap of all your winnings
And risk it on one turn of pitch-and-toss,
And lose, and start again at your beginnings
And never breathe a word about your loss;
If you can force your heart and nerve and sinew
To serve your turn long after they are gone,
And so hold on when there is nothing in you
Except the Will which says to them: "Hold on!"
If you can talk with crowds and keep your virtue,
Or walk with kings—nor lose the common touch,
If neither foes nor loving friends can hurt you,
If all men count with you, but none too much;
If you can fill the unforgiving minute
With sixty seconds' worth of distance run—
Yours is the Earth and everything that's in it,
And—which is more—you'll be a Man, my son!

Rudyard Kipling

CASA HOGAR LOS ANGELITOS (CHLA), a non-profit civil association in Mexico, is funded through the Children's Foundation (FEED Scholarship Fund and Children's Foundation) a 501(c)(3) non-profit organization located in Loveland, Colorado. If you would like to contribute to one of the programs of CHLA, receive additional information, or make a "vision" trip to visit this program, please send your contributions or requests to

THE CHILDREN'S FOUNDATION
P.O. Box 1443
Loveland, CO 80539
www.tcfcares.org

Profits received from the sale of this book go towards the general operation and expansion program of The Children's Foundation and Casa Hogar Los Angelitos.

CPSIA information can be obtained
at www.ICGtesting.com
Printed in the USA
FSOW03n1139230417
33345FS